Axure for Mobile, Second Edition

Axure for Mobile, Second Edition

Building Mobile Prototypes with Axure RP 7.0

v1.04

Lennart Hennigs

Published by

Lennart Hennigs

Ditfurthstraße 55

33611 Bielefeld, Germany

mail@lennarthennigs.de

Für Steffi und Ida.

Foreword

I moved from static wireframes to Axure a couple years ago and haven't looked back. The ability to show clients and users what the experience would be, right on the phone has been invaluable. Taking those same artifacts and exploring the design further and collaborating with the development teams has facilitated rapid iterations and clarity in communications, coupled with the ability to generate design documents.

It wasn't until Axure 6.5 that you could really be productive when prototyping for mobile, and that's when Lennart wrote the first version of this book. It's full of references, of recipes for how to achieve key tasks, and the philosophy of mobile.

When I picked up version 1, I was hoping to get a tidbit or two for me, and an organized way to bring my team up to speed with the techniques of Axure for mobile. What I got was so much more: nearly every section about Axure contained something of interest: improving Axure's CSS output, how to configure prototypes for each type of mobile device, and of course, step by step instructions on the fundamental technique for prototyping mobile apps: panel-based prototypes.

Axure 7 has added a lot more mobile capabilities, particularly adaptive layouts, push/pull widgets, and variables for panel states. Lennart has added information for the best use of all of these, and over 200 refreshed screenshots to make it easy to follow.

If you've gotten past the Axure basics and want to really prototype for mobile devices, you need this book. Take your time with it, and come back to it often.

I do.

Barbara Ballard
Chicago, Illinois, USA

Axure for Mobile, Second Edition

Contents

1. Introduction

Thank you for spending money on me – well, on this book, that is. I hope that it proves to be money well spent.

This book distills my experiences of building mobile prototypes with Axure. It offers tried and tested best practices that will make your prototyping life easier. After reading this book, you'll understand how to design for mobile. You'll know what steps to take to create mobile website and app prototypes. But this book will also help with non-mobile projects, as it teaches you how to build common interaction patterns in Axure. I hope this book will find a permanent place on your desk as an invaluable guide.

Introduction To The Second Edition

Writing this book was quite an interesting experience. I never planned to write a book in the first place.

It started with me showing friends and colleagues Axure's mobile capabilities of Axure 6.0. At first I only had a couple of notes which evolved over time into a small slide deck. But people kept asking me questions – "How do I do this…?" – so I kept adding slides.

Along the way I discovered a couple of new ways to solve common problems, so I jotted them down, planning to post them on my blog or in the Axure forum. But suddenly my notes exceeded 30 pages and I still had a long list of things I wanted to explore.

Then Axure 6.5 came out, which was the first real mobile-friendly version. So I thought: let's turn this into a small book. But I failed miserably because the content resulted in quite a big book, spanning 213 pages.

As a nice side-effect I learned even more about Axure, and quite a bit about HTML5 and jQuery. I learned to write comfortably on a train (where I did and still do most of my writing) and that it is actually easy to find the time to do the things you want to do – like writing a book.

But I am still mastering the skill of recognizing when I start boring my friends with random Axure-nerdiness.

I also met and talked to a bunch of interesting and fun people all over the world and I am always surprised by the spirit and kindness of the Axure community. And I never expected that people would read the stuff I write. But you do. So thanks for this.

Why Write a New Version

With version 7.0 Axure got a (much needed) UI overhaul. In addition, new functionality that makes prototyping even easier was added, for example the possibility to push and pull content or the 'fit to browser' option for *dynamic panels*. I thus had to update the book to reflect these changes. Also a couple of the how to chapters needed to be rewritten. I added new patterns to show how Axure's new capabilities can be put to use. I updated the 'Scrolling', 'Swiping', 'Dialogs and Popups', 'Text Fields and Forms', 'Sticky Headers for Lists', 'Splash Screens' and 'Sliding Menus' chapters and added the 'Tabs', 'Accordion Lists', 'Drag to Refresh' and 'Fullscreen on Scroll' chapters. I redid parts of the 'Viewing Your Prototype' chapter and wrote a new 'Adaptive Views' chapter explaining how to create responsive prototypes. Last but not least, I did some housekeeping, updating the links and the information in all chapters.

About This Book

This book explains how to design mobile and pad-based prototypes of apps and web pages, how to build typical mobile UI patterns and how to view your prototypes on mobile devices. It teaches you how to prepare Axure for mobile prototyping. It explains how to document your prototypes and it will equip you with quite a few Axure tips and tricks.

All major mobile platforms (iOS, Android, Windows Phone and Firefox OS) are covered. Their capabilities and the impact on mobile prototyping are explained. Topics specific to mobile web design are also mentioned.

How This Book is Organized

The first three chapters contain background information on mobile interaction design. The chapter 'Mobile Design Basics' explains the constraints and requirements of mobile applications and websites. 'Designing for Mobile' describes the steps of a best-practice design process. The 'On Prototyping' chapter offers details and best practices for building prototypes.

This is followed by the 'real meat' of the book – the chapters dealing with Axure itself: 'Setting up Axure' explains how to prepare Axure for your mobile prototyping endeavors. I highly recommend that you read this chapter before jumping ahead. The 'Building Mobile Prototypes' chapter explains the different options for constructing a mobile prototype. 'Viewing Your Prototype' teaches you how to prepare your prototype for different viewing options you will encounter on the different mobile platforms.

The chapters 'Prototyping Interactions', 'Mobile UI Patterns', 'Advanced Topics' and 'Adaptive Views' are the central chapters of this book. They explain in depth how to prototype mobile user experiences. 'Creating Documentation' teaches you how to generate different types of specification for your Axure prototype.

Last but not least, there are two additional chapters 'Appendix I – Best Practices' and 'Appendix II – Tips and Tricks' where you can pick up a few Axure tips.

Who This Book is For

Do you have a great idea for a mobile website or an app? Want to turn this idea into a reality? Are you looking for a fast way to test different concepts before committing to one of them? Do you want to present your idea to your stakeholders to let them experience it before development starts? And do you want to showcase it on a mobile device?

If you answered any of those questions with yes, this book is for you. It doesn't matter what fancy title you have on your business card, or whether you work in Marketing, Sales, Development or as a designer.

Axure is a prototyping tool, allowing you to test your assumptions and showcase your ideas and concepts. Specifications will become less important in your workflow as you can now show and tell your app's (or website's) intended experience.

Before Getting Started

Some basic knowledge about Axure is beneficial to get the most out of this book. In addition, some basic knowledge about 'your' mobile platform is helpful, but the book provides resources and links to help you get you started on both topics.

To get the most out of Axure, don't shy away from some basic programming concepts like conditional logic [102] (a.k.a. 'IF … THEN … ELSE' statements) and variables. You'll need them to turn your static wireframes into interactive prototypes that can react to and work with user input. I offer some tips on how to work with conditions and variables in Axure in 'Appendix I – Best Practices' chapter.

Axure's (Mobile) Capabilities

This section does not replace the release notes [103] or the product details page of Axure RP 7.0. Instead, I want to give you a quick overview of what you currently can and cannot do with Axure. After reading this section you will be able to decide if Axure is the right prototyping tool for you.

What It Can Do

Axure allows you to create mobile wireframes and link them together to create User Interface (UI) Flows. You can modify your screens' content and create interactive prototypes. You can turn wireframes into high-fidelity screens by using UI libraries. You can make its HTML output mobile-friendly and view it on a mobile device. Axure can detect and work with touch gestures and allows you to prototype animations and transitions.

With Axure 7.0 you can create responsive prototypes. Its responsive design approach is currently the smartest on the market. You can set up different views via breakpoints and define how your UI elements should look in these views. You can now also detect and work with your device's orientation.

What Is Still Missing

Axure does not support multi-touch gestures. It's HTML output is not suited for building a real product and you cannot edit it easily.

Examples and Resources

All examples of this book are available online. You can find the download link for the .rp file in the 'The Axure Source File' chapter in the end of the book.

In this book you'll find quite a few links referring you to articles and other online resources. To make these links accessible in the printed version, I've used bit.ly, a URL shortening service, and a numbering system: each external link is followed by a three digit number in brackets. You can access the links using the following URL schema:

```
http://bit.ly/a4m_[EnterYourNumberHere]
```

On the book's companion site you'll find additional links to resources, news on Axure and much more:

```
http://www.axureformobile.com
```

If you have any questions, suggestions or feedback don't hesitate to contact me via e-mail. I want to hear what you think and how your (mobile) projects are going.

And I have one final thing to ask: please take a minute or two to review this book on Amazon. Your review makes a difference, as it provides other Axure users with an informed opinion. Thank you!

2. Mobile Design Basics

This chapter provides a quick introduction to the basics of mobile app design. If you are a seasoned mobile veteran feel free to skim and skip this chapter. To keep this chapter as short as possible I moved links to additional information to the footnotes. Please refer to them if you want to find out more about a particular topic.

Context of Use

When designing for mobile you have to remember that users expect the same level of user experience from mobiles as from desktop computers. They even expect similar performance – in terms of speed and network connectivity.[1]

Not too long ago (in 2007, that is, before the iPhone) mobile devices where good at a very limited number of things (mainly calling) – and were used when people were on the go. But the iPhone changed this. Josh Clark explains that the mobile context (as such) is nowadays a myth.[2] People use their mobile devices everywhere for a wide range of tasks[3] – guessing what features people need or expect, based on the device they use, is a flawed and outdated concept, says Clark. However, people might be on the go, distracted and interrupted while using their smartphone.

Mobile Operating Systems

Another aspect to consider when designing for mobile is today's operating system (OS) fragmentation.

There are currently five major smartphone platforms competing for market share:

- Apple's iOS
- Google's Android
- Microsoft's Windows Phone.
- Firefox OS
- RIM's Blackberry OS.

Android is the biggest player in terms of market share – but there are no exact numbers; they depend on the statistic you look at. Below are two examples: the first statistic by MillenialMedia [104] is based on mobile ads visits and the second one by Gartner [105] is based on (real and estimated) worldwide sales:

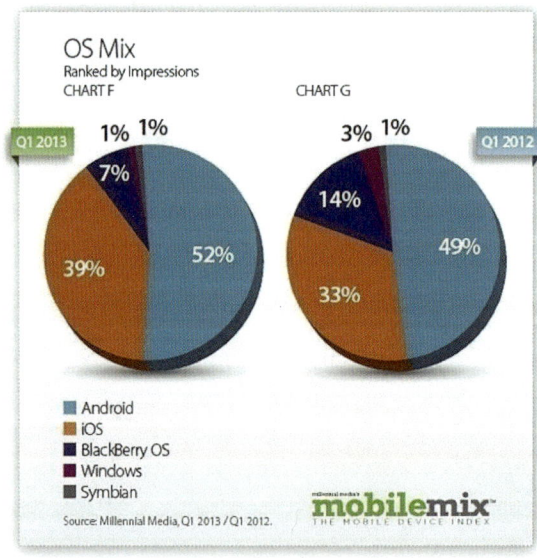

Worldwide Smartphone Sales to End Users by Operating System in 1Q13 (Thousands of Units)

Operating System	1Q13 Units	1Q13 Market Share (%)	1Q12 Units	1Q12 Market Share (%)
Android	156,186.0	74.4	83,684.4	56.9
iOS	38,331.8	18.2	33,120.5	22.5
BlackBerry	6,218.6	3.0	9,939.3	6.8
Microsoft	5,989.2	2.9	2,722.5	1.9
Bada	1,370.8	0.7	3,843.7	2.6
Symbian	1,349.4	0.6	12,466.9	8.5
Others	600.3	0.3	1,242.9	0.8
Total	**210,046.1**	**100.0**	**147,020.2**	**100.0**

Source: Gartner (May 2013)

But OS fragmentation also refers to the different OS versions in use. This mainly applies to Google's OS because there are quite a few Android versions currently in use.

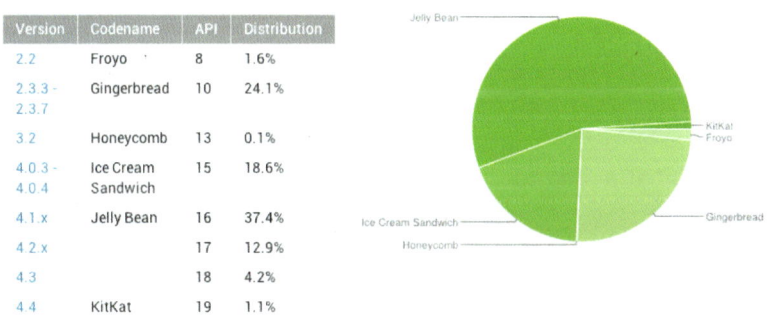

Version	Codename	API	Distribution
2.2	Froyo	8	1.6%
2.3.3 - 2.3.7	Gingerbread	10	24.1%
3.2	Honeycomb	13	0.1%
4.0.3 - 4.0.4	Ice Cream Sandwich	15	18.6%
4.1.x	Jelly Bean	16	37.4%
4.2.x		17	12.9%
4.3		18	4.2%
4.4	KitKat	19	1.1%

Data collected during a 7-day period ending on December 2, 2013.
Any versions with less than 0.1% distribution are not shown.

In December 2013 25% of all Android devices still run a version of Android 2.x.[4] This number is important because with Android 4.0 (released 10/2011), quite a few user interface paradigms were changed. In addition phone vendors change the Android user interface to create their own user experience, making designing for Android even more complex.[5] Sony's or Samsung's version of Android differs from Google's 'vanilla' one.

On iOS this problem is almost nonexistent since iPhone and iPad users update their devices shortly after an update becomes available.[6] And since Apple is the only vendor of iOS a uniform user experience is ensured.

Mobile Constraints

Mobile devices share several constraints compared to 'regular' computers: they come in various screen resolutions and sizes. They offer limited screen estate and provide different input and output mechanisms. Mobiles vary in their performance and you cannot rely on a good network reception or on the quality of their Internet connection – they are after all mobile devices. This is why Luke Wroblewski suggests designing for 'Mobile First' to force you to focus and 'sharpen' the scope of your design before starting to design for other screens.[7]

Screen Resolutions

There is a wide range of screen resolutions and sizes available on mobiles phones (resulting in different dots per inch (dpi) values), yet the majority of smartphones share the same physical size.[8] Current mobile devices can operate in portrait and landscape mode. There are even different interaction paradigms and UI patterns available for the different orientations.[9]

As stated before, Android devices offer the most variety. The picture below is from a Hong Kong mobile app agency that uses about 400 different Android devices in its quality assurance testing.[10]

On iOS you only need to remember that devices have either a non-retina or a retina display, as the latter offers twice the resolution. Non-retina iPhones (all iPhones until the iPhone 3GS) offer 320x480px display and retina iPhones have a 640x960px screen. With the iPhone 5 Apple introduced a larger retina display (640x1136px). The same logic applies to the iPad and to the iPad mini (1024x768px vs. 2048x1536px). These two diagrams by OpenSignal [106] show the range of device resolutions of Android and iOS:

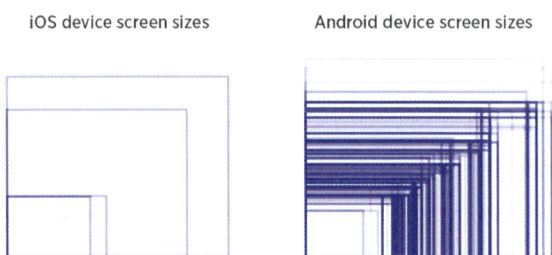

Designing for Windows Phone and Firefox OS is easier because there are fewer devices available.

Screen Estate

Due to their dimensions, mobile screens display less information compared to computer screens, yet the information needs to be larger to be legible. Content also needs to be more condensed – text must be shorter and more to the point; images need to be smaller to fit the screen.[11] Plus you need to take into account that complex information seems to be harder to understand on small screens.[12]

Limited screen estate is also one reason why the structure of mobile apps needs to be simpler compared to their computer counterparts.[13] Quite a few apps even offer all of their functionality on a single screen.

Input Mechanisms

Most modern smartphones now only feature a touch screen (and a few hardware keys) but there are still a lot of mobiles offering additional input mechanisms like cursor keys, full keyboards, trackballs, stylus or pen input out there.

Regardless of the input mechanism, mobile devices are not great for entering large amounts of text or performing precision tasks. That's why you want to reduce text entry and give your users a smart set of defaults instead. Try to reduce the number of clicks necessary to complete a task and make the most important functions visible and easy to access. UI elements of mobile apps need to be larger (compared to their desktop computer counterparts) to make it hard to miss them visually and interaction-wise. When designing for touch interaction, clickable areas need to be about a square centimeter in size (to suit our fingertips).

Touch interfaces have also made it popular to directly interact with content, like using the 'pinch' gesture to zoom.[14] That's why you'll see less UI elements in modern interfaces: the content becomes the interface.[15] But the reduction of UI elements introduced new challenges: how to show your app's functionality to your users? You can use metaphors in your design and use established interaction paradigms in your user interface. In addition, try to use UI elements that communicate their purpose clearly.[16]

Mobile user interfaces make heavy use of animations and transitions to help users understand what is happening on the screen. New elements scroll in and out of view and transitions provide some orientation, e.g. screens in a wizard come in from the right, detail screens are zoomed in, etc.[17]

For more information on mobile interaction design take a look at an excerpt [108] from Rachel Hinman's book 'The Mobile Frontier' [209] and Dan Saffer's book 'Gestural Interfaces' [210].

For a well-phrased critique of todays touch interfaces take a look at Bret Victor's articles called 'A brief rant on the future of Interaction Design' [109].

Mobile Advantages

Despite these constraints, there are several advantages offered by mobile devices: users can create and play back different types of content (images, audio, video and text) anywhere. Mobiles are touch-based and can detect motion – new ways of interaction (gestures, shaking or tilting the device) are being introduced on mobiles. They can detect and utilize the users' physical location. Mobile devices are personal – they belong to a single user, they are always carried by their owners and (almost) always on.

Based on these advantages, Toni Ahonen considers mobiles to be the seventh mass media after the printing press, recordings, cinema, radio, TV and the Internet.[18]

Take-aways

These are the key things you should remember when designing for mobile:

- Users expect mobile performance to be similar to their desktop experiences.
- You cannot guess the users' tasks or their context of use just because they are using a mobile device.
- You need to design for different screen sizes and orientations.
- You might have to design for different operating systems and OS versions.

- Mobile apps have a reduced feature set – good ones are more focused, offering only the most relevant use cases to their users.
- Due to the reduced feature set, the navigation and structure of a mobile app or website is simpler.
- Your app's content needs to be tailored to the smaller screen.
- Information must be legible and elements must be large enough for touch interaction.
- Make data entry and navigation within your app or your website easy.
- Place more focus on your apps's or website's content.
- Use animations and transitions to show the user what is happening.
- Keep the mobile advantages in mind: location detection and use, media creation, etc.

Now you know what makes mobile design different. Let's discuss next what steps to take when designing for mobile.

---

[1] See mobile [002] and tablet user [003] expectations regarding loading speed of websites.

[2] See Josh Clark's presentation 'The Myths of Mobile Context' [004] and the summary by Anthony Wing Kosner 'Seven Deadly Mobile Myths: Josh Clark Debunks the Desktop Paradigm and More' [005].

[3] For more insights and data on mobile usage visit Google's 'Our Mobile Planet' [006] or mobiThinking's statistics collection [007].

[4] Data taken from 'Android's Developer Dashboard' [008] that is updated bi-weekly. OpenSignalMaps also provide a nice overview over Android's device fragmentation in their article 'The many faces of a little green robot' [009].

[5] For more information on the different Android vendors see the Joe Wilcox article 'Google has lost control of Android' [010].

[6] See for example the data Chitika published on the iOS 6 adoption rate [012] for North America.

[7] Read 'Mobile First: What does it mean?' [013] by Riley Graham to get an overview over the topic. Luke Wroblewski's has published a book of the same name: 'Mobile First' [014]. There is also a video [016] of one of Luke's talks online. For additional resources please take a look at Luke's article 'Multi-

Device Web Design: An Evolution' [017]. For a detailed discussion of the mobile first concept take a look at Joshua Johnson's article 'Mobile First Design: Why It's Great and Why It Sucks' [019].

For more details on the principles and patterns of multi-screen user experiences check out the (German) page of Wolfram Nagel and Valentin Fischer called 'Multiscreen Experience' [018].

[8] For more details on mobile devices and dpi values take a look at Travis Hines' article 'Designing (and converting) for multiple mobile densities' [020]. For a collection of different screen sizes visit 'www.screensiz.es/' [021].

[9] If you want to find out more about orientation-based design, read the excellent article: 'Designing For Device Orientation: From Portrait To Landscape' [022] by Avi Itzkovitch.

[10] See Techcrunch's article [023] and Animoca's own article [024] on their Android QA-testing portfolio. AppBrain [025] also publish the Android OS information of their user base.

[11] For mobile web sites you might even want to provide your images in different sizes. For more information read Mat Marquis article 'Responsive Images: How they Almost Worked and What We Need' [026].

[12] 'Mobile Content is Twice as Difficult' [027] to understand, says Jakob Nielsen.

[13] Giles Colborne explains in his great book 'Simple and Usable' [218] that simpler does not mean providing a 'dumbed-down' user experience.

[14] See Luke Wroblewski's 'Touch Gesture Reference Guide' [029] for an overview over common used gestures.

[15] For more information on content becoming the interface see Steven Poole's blog post 'Against Chrome: A Manifesto' [030].

[16] For more information on affordances (a term coined by Don Norman) see his essay 'Affordances and Design' [033] and the presentation 'Affordances in Modern Web Design' [032] by Andrew Maier.

[17] For more information on the use of transitions check out the web site 'Meaningful Transitions' [034]. Good articles on the topic are 'Mission Transition' [035] by Mark Cossey and 'Storyboarding iPad Transitions' [036] by Greg Nudelman.

[18] See Toni Ahonen's article 'Deeper insights into the 7th Mass Media channel' [037].

3. Designing for Mobile

Explaining how to best design a mobile app (or a website) in detail is beyond the scope of this book, but I want to walk you through the key steps and point you to additional information.

With the sheer amount of mobile applications available your product faces steep competition. A successful app or website combines three traits: First, it addresses a specific need a user group has. Its functionality focuses solely on solving this need. Second, it fits perfectly with the mobile platform it is running on – users know how to use it 'intuitively' because they recognize interaction paradigms they have learned before. And last but not least, a successful app or website 'stands out from the crowd' – this could be through its set of functions, the use cases it solves, its visual design or through good use of animations and transitions. To create such an app or website, take the following steps.

Know your OS

Familiarize yourself with the Human Interface Guidelines (HIG) of 'your' mobile operating system. This will prove to be time well spent, because the HIGs describe in detail how to design apps that 'fit' their mobile platform. An app that adheres to its platform guidelines will seem more 'intuitive', since its users are already familiar with the UI elements it uses.

Here are links to the different mobile HIGs:

- iOS [202]
- Android [187]
- Windows Phone [203]
- Firefox OS [224]
- Blackberry 10 [205]

Also take a look at mobile UI pattern galleries and UI libraries that showcase best practices for common UI design problems. There are books available that solely focus on mobile design patterns: 'Mobile Design Pattern Gallery' [206] by Theresa Neil and 'Designing Mobile Interfaces' [207] by Steven Hoober and Eric Berkman. The book 'Smashing Android UI' [208] by Juhani Lehtimäki offers a good introduction to the Android user interface paradigms.

A mobile website is also quite different from a 'regular' website. Check out the '10 Ways Mobile Sites are Different from Desktop Web Sites' [117] article by Shanshan Ma and 'What Websites can Learn From Mobile' [118] by Michael Wilson for more information.

Know Your Users

Base the design of your app or website on your target audience – on their needs, expectations and knowledge.

As stated before, your solution must solve a specific need of your targeted users – maybe in a novel way or with a good choice of functions. The better your solution fits their expectations and needs of your users the better they will be able to use it – and the better they'll like it.

Your users' knowledge about mobile devices and their skills will impact your design. If they are novice users, they will be happy with pre-defined flows (e.g. wizards) and with a limited number of choices. You can offer experienced users more freedom and use advanced interaction mechanisms (like multi-touch gestures) since they will most likely know, expect and use them.

A popular way to capture insights into your users are personas.[1] A persona is a human-friendly format for user-related facts. It distills the information about a specific user group into a fictitious user profile.

For more information on personas take a look at Neil Turner's article 'Getting the most out of personas' [110] and at the book 'The Essential Persona Lifecycle' [211] by John Pruitt and Tamara Adlin.

User scenarios, describing a sequence of events, often accompany a persona description. They offer insights into the motivation, knowledge and capabilities of a persona. Scenarios often mention tools and objects a persona uses.

For more information on user scenarios check out the article 'Using Scenarios' [111] by Jax Wechsler and the book 'Storytelling for User Experience' by Whitney Quesenbery and Kevin Brooks.

Use personas and user scenarios to capture what you know about your targeted users. Use them as your reference and try to design for your users solving their problems.

Create a Product Vision

Write down one or two sentences describing the solution you want to create. This will be your product vision statement.

A good example is the product vision of Metro, the Visual Design Language of Windows Phone 7.[2]

> METRO IS OUR DESIGN LANGUAGE. WE CALL IT METRO BECAUSE IT'S MODERN AND CLEAN. IT'S FAST AND IN MOTION. IT'S ABOUT CONTENT AND TYPOGRAPHY. AND IT'S ENTIRELY AUTHENTIC.

A good product vision consists of the following ingredients:
- the target audience and their needs
- the product category
- the key functionality and the major benefits
- current practice/competition and key differentiators and
- maybe some drivers.

For more information on how to create a product vision take a look at James Shore's online book chapter 'The Art of Agile Development: Vision' [112] and the article 'The 3 Steps for Creating an Experience Vision' [113] by Jared Spool.

Create Design Tenets

Next, create a handful of design tenets based on your product vision. Design tenets are short phrases that describe the product vision and the targeted user experience in more detail.[3] They will offer guidance when you need to select the best fitting option out of several possible choices – they help you make design decisions. Their purpose is to be your guiding light – showing you the path forward by reminding you of your targeted user experience.

Here are the design tenets of Metro and the first design tenet in more detail:

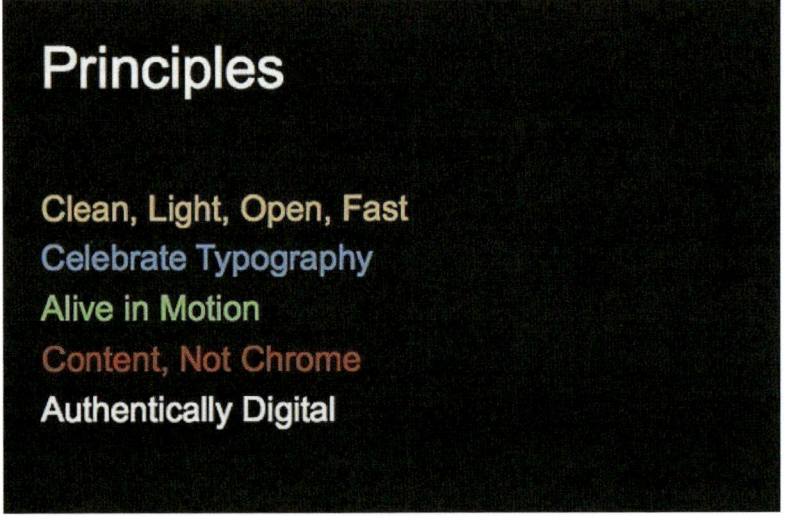

It is important that you make your design tenets 'sticky': print them out, post them to your walls and hand them to your clients – you want to make them visible.[4] Good design tenets are specific to your project, concrete, non-ambiguous, catchy and describe differentiating properties (and not single features) of your product.

For more information on design tenets see 'Design Principles in a Nutshell' [114] by Leah Buley, '(Design) Principles to Build By' [115] by Stephen P. Anderson and 'Creating Great Design Principles: 6 Counter-intuitive Tests' [116] by Jared Spool.

Last but not least, here is the result of Microsoft's design vision, the UI style of Windows Phone:

You can see how their product vision is reflected in their user interface.

Keep Your Axe Sharp

Prototyping is a craft (more on this in the next chapter) and since you are reading this you probably plan to add Axure to your toolbox. Spend some time watching the tutorials Axure offers [119] and browse through its forum [120] to see how other people use Axure. To get to know Axure (or any other new prototyping tool) Jared Spool suggests redoing a project you did before [121], to help you learn the differences.

It is also important to understand the strengths and shortcomings of Axure (see 'Axure's Mobile Capabilities'). With this knowledge you can identify what functionality will be complex to prototype and how well Axure will be able support you. You might even decide that Axure is not the right tool this time around.

Create a Concept

Start by recapping your idea. Look at your product vision and the design tenets you created and review your personas and the user scenarios. Think about the different use cases your app needs to support to make your targeted users 'happy'. Decide what functions are needed to fulfill the most important use cases.

Next, consider three aspects of your solution before you start prototyping: its information architecture, the interaction paradigms you are going to use and the visual design you want to apply.

Information Architecture

Here are some questions related to your solution's information architecture (IA):

- How will your users get from A to B?
- Will people need to take the same 'path' through your app or will you provide shortcuts?
- Will your app offer a fixed main screen or will your users be able to customize it to their liking?

One way to visualize your solutions's structure is using an Information Architecture Diagram.[5] An IA diagram provides a high-level overview over your app or website. It shows the (key) screens and how they relate to each other. Think of an IA diagram as the 'floor plan' of your app. The easiest way to create an IA diagram is to sketch a couple of boxes (one for each screen), label and connect them. See a sample IA diagram below.[6]

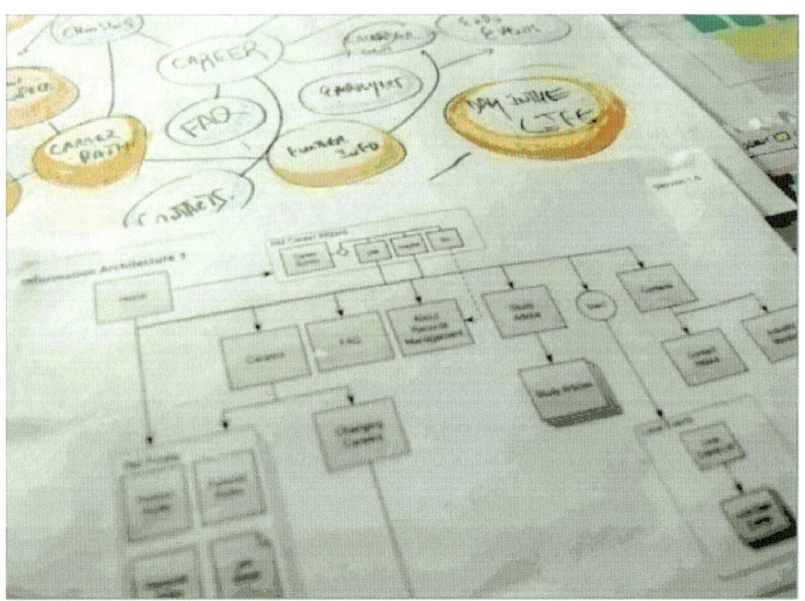

There are a quite few IA diagram notations available that you can use. Take a look at Jesse James Garrett's 'Visual Vocabulary' [122] or at Jakub Linowski's 'Interactive Sketching Notation' [123].

For more information on IA diagrams take a look at the book 'Communicating Design' by Dan M. Brown (that also covers other UX artifacts), read Luke Wroblewski's article on 'Application Maps' [052] and read the summary of Peter Sikking's talk 'Mobile Before and After January 9th, 2007' [124]. In the article 'Designing for Mobile, Part 1: Information Architecture' [125] Elaine McVicar describes different IA patterns of mobile applications.

Interaction Design

Next, think about the interaction paradigms you are going to use:

- How are you going to offer the solution's functionality to your users?
- Will you use 'traditional' UI elements like buttons or lists or will you also use touch-only interaction paradigms, like gestures?

- How do you communicate the different interaction mechanisms to your users?
- What are the different options for implementing a function and which one is best suited for your solution?
- What UI patterns are you going to use?

These questions can be answered with wireframes and user interface flows. Wireframes depict the layout of a user interface. They describe the structure, content and behavior of a single screen (or parts of it); its visual design is not in focus. Wireframes show the relationship and hierarchy of the page elements. They explain the interactive elements, their relationship to each other and how the user will get feedback. They also contain some (sample) content of the solution.

A user interface flow is a set of wireframes visualizing an 'interaction path'; highlighting what interface elements are used (e.g. a tap or a gesture) and how the system responds (e.g. with animations, transitions, pop-up dialogs, showing the next screen). Different pathways are often visualized to showcase important variations of the user interface (e.g. error cases). UI flows are one key deliverable of mobile interaction design (other than the prototype itself).

While IA diagrams provide a high-level overview of a solution, wireframes illustrates the content of the different screens and UI flows show its 'pathways'.

For more information on wireframes and UI flows see Bryan Rieger's 'Modeling the Mobile User Experience' [126] presentation and Nick Finck's 'Mobile Information Architecture and Interaction Design' [127] presentation. A good article on (digital) wireframes is '10 simple ways to make wireframes more useful' [128] by Steve Cable.

Visual Design

Last but not least, you want to define how your solution will look. One thing to consider is whether you want to use a certain metaphor or a skeuomorph (a terrible word, I know – I'll explain it in a second) in your solution. Known and accepted metaphors in UI design are for example your computer's desktop, the shopping basket or the wooden bookshelf of reading applications. Joel Spolsky offers a good introduction to metaphors in his article 'Affordances and Metaphors' [129]. A skeuomorph is "a derivative object that retains ornamental design cues to a structure that was necessary in the original."[7] Good examples are Apple's iOS Cards app to create postcards (it looks like a postcard) or the Calendar app for Mac (it looked like a leather-bound calendar before Mavericks).

For more information on skeuomorphs see Christian Holst's article 'Designing with Skeuomorphs' [131].

But use these concepts carefully because they can also cause 'harm'. The wrong metaphor can confuse users and over-doing a skeuomorph leads to 'UI kitsch' that will repel certain users.

> "Leather buttons, stitches, torn paper edges, multi-screen multi-column pseudo-newspaper layouts... on the screen it is just kitsch. Kitsch, as in: it tries to be something that it is not – and miserably fails at the attempt: Paper doesn't wear down in the digital dimension. There are no leather buttons in the real world. Meaningless stitches in the UI distract the eye from the information. [...]
>
> The same rule applies to visual metaphors: Just as with any literary metaphor, a visual metaphor hurts if it doesn't clarify; it breaks if you stretch it; it becomes ludicrous if you combine it with a second or third metaphor."
>
> Oliver Reichenstein
> Designing for iPad: Reality Check [130]

Another aspect to consider is whether you want to use the default look and feel of the OS you are developing for, or if you want to create your own look and feel. Custom UI elements are harder to implement but they can differentiate your app from its competition.[8]

To get some inspiration for your solution's visual design, review well-rated apps and take a look at UI galleries.

Start Sketching

When you start designing your app or website you want to get your ideas out of your head as quickly as possible. You want to go for quantity and to explore different concepts. That's why I recommend to start designing on paper. Grab a pen and sketch your ideas.

The nice thing about paper is that you'll be really fast. You won't grow too attached to your sketches, which makes it easier for you to discard the ones that are not good enough. Sketches look rough and unfinished thus making it easy for people to give feedback because they see it's a work-in-progress. As mobile screens are small, paper allows you to put all your concepts next to each other, allowing you to get a complete overview.

One of the best presentations on how to get started with sketching is by Leah Buley, called 'Good Design Faster' [132]. There she suggests to sketch several variations of a single screen to explore different ideas (using a so-called 6-up template).[9] After discussing the pros and cons of each concept, combine the best ideas into one single concept. Afterwards you can explore different metaphors for your solution and evaluate different interaction paradigms for selected functions.

After you have created a few key screens you can 'zoom out' by spelling out your first use cases and create the first UI flows on paper. Or you can start with an IA diagram and then 'zoom in' and sketch individual screens.

Both approaches work equally well, top-down or bottom-up – it's a matter of personal preference. See what works best for you. I describe this topic in more detail in my article 'Sketching For Better Mobile Experiences' [139].

A good article on sketching is 'Sketching: the Visual Thinking Power Tool' [133] by Mike Rohde. And besides Leah Buley's presentation 'Good Design Faster' [132], Jackson Fox's presentation 'Sketching for Interface Design 101' [134] and 'The Art of Sketching Interfaces' [135] by Jason Mesut and Sam Smith is also worth a look. A great book on the topic is 'Sketching User Experiences: The Workbook' [212] by Saul Greenberg and Bill Buxton.

If you are looking for mobile wireframe inspiration, take a look at the 'Inspiring UI Wireframe Sketches' [136] article by Gisele Muller, visit 'moobileframes' [137], a blog dedicated to showcasing mobile wireframe sketches and have a look at Jakub Linowski's 'Wireframe Magazine' [138].

Continue in Axure

After some iterations you will want to transfer your sketches into Axure because certain aspects of your solution will be hard to convey on paper, for example how the animations and page transitions should work, or to see how much content will really fit onto your screens.

Start by creating key screens. You want to see how they look and if the content and the interactive elements fit. After you have created a few of them, 'wire them together' creating your first UI flows. Or you can import your hand-drawn sketches to get a first impression of your concept.[10]

Evaluate and Iterate

An important step, which you want to do alongside the others, is to frequently check if the assumptions you base your design upon are still valid. Evaluate your concept every time you evolve it. Depending on the topic and your scope you can test your ideas with people that are part of your targeted user group or with your peers:

- 'Pitch' your product vision to potential users to see if it is concise, understandable and compelling.
- Explain your design tenets and the key functionality to potential users and peers to see if they agree to your solution's scope.
- Show your peers your first design sketches to get feedback.
- Compare your information architecture with apps you like or with apps your solution will compete with.
- Check if the interaction paradigms you use are in line with the operating system's Human Interface Guidelines. (See the 'Know your Mobile Platform' chapter for more details.)

- Try to find the core of your concept and to cut all unnecessary elements.[11] When in doubt about which elements to keep and which to take out, take a look at your design tenets and the insights of your target user group to help you decide.
- And prototype different variations of your concepts to see which works best.

As you have seen, Axure is not the first thing to start with when you begin a mobile project. The other steps are essential to get your solution's design right.

If you want to find out more about mobile design and development, I highly recommend the following books: 'Tapworthy' [213] by Josh Clark, 'Mobile Design and Development' [214] by Brian Fling, 'Designing the iPhone User Experience' [215] by Suzanne Ginsburg and 'The Mobile Frontier' [209] by Rachel Hinman.

---

[1] Alan Cooper first described personas in his book 'The Inmates are running the Asylum' [219].

[2] Or rather: 'The Design Language formerly known as Metro' [039], as of August 2012. Images are taken from A. Shum's presentation 'Designing Windows Phone 7' Series (video [040] & presentation [041], .ppt - 14mb).
A nice summary of the Metro principles provides Connor Turnbull in his article 'Emulating Microsoft's Metro Design Language' [042].

[3] I use the term 'tenets' to differentiate project-specific from general design principles like the 'Golden Ratio' or other design and UX rules like Bruce 'Tog' Tognazzini's 'First Principles of Interaction Design' [043] or Dieter Rams' 'Ten Principles for Good Design' [044].

[4] The Heath brothers explain in their book 'Made to Stick. Why Some Ideas Survive and Others Die' [220] principles that make ideas and concepts easy to remember. For a one-page summary take a look at the 'Success Model' overview [046].

[5] For web sites IA diagrams are often called 'Sitemaps', for desktop apps I found the term 'Application Maps' [052].

[6] Thanks to Gary Barber for sharing his UX pictures [053].

[7] Wikipedia has a good article [054] on skeuomorphs.

[8] One app shop renowned for its custom UI is 'Tapbots' [055] – my favorite app from them is 'Tweetbot' [056], a twitter client.

[9] There are quite a few mobile sketching templates [057] available. My favorite iPhone template is by Erik Loehfelm [058].

[10] On iOS there is now an app for making sketches interactive called P.O.P. [059] With it you can to take pictures of your sketches and link them together on your iPhone.

[11] Good books on designing for simplicity are John Maeda's 'The Laws of Simplicity' [221] and Giles Colborne's 'Simple and Usable' [218].

4. On Prototyping

Axure is a powerful prototyping tool. You can create (sketchy-looking) wireframes as well as fully interactive prototypes that can come close to the user experience of a real application or website.

Why Prototype?

Even though you have this much prototyping power at your fingertips, prototyping is not an end in itself. A prototype should help you gain an understanding of a design problem. It can also be a means to show your concepts to others (clients, product managers, developers, your peers, etc.) or help you explain certain aspects of your design and get feedback.

Questions that will help you focus your prototyping efforts are:
- What do I already know about the product?
- What do I want to find out?
- What aspects of my design do I want to communicate?
- What aspects do I need to get feedback on? On the structure of the app? On its interaction paradigms? On the content of its key screens? On its visual design?
- What are the (key) use cases I need to show in my prototype?

A Prototype's Fidelity

The fidelity of your prototype depends on the answers to the questions above. A prototype's level of fidelity consists of three dimensions: its 'depth', its level of interactivity, and its visual design. Use these dimensions to determine the appropriate 'fidelity mix' for your prototype.

Depth

The 'depth' of a prototype refers to its navigation hierarchy – the number of screens you include in your prototype and the level of detail you provide for the screens.

A 'horizontal' prototype provides an overview of all key screens but doesn't show each screen in full detail. It showcases all major areas of the app or website to be designed.

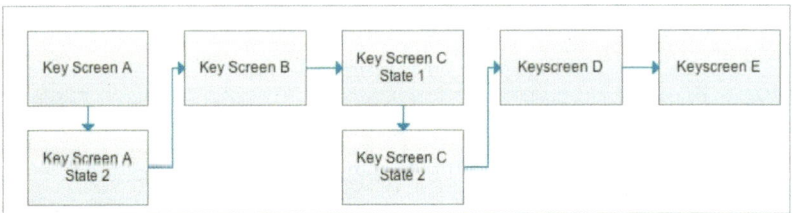

A 'vertical' prototype focuses on a few selected use cases and shows them in more detail. They are used to showcase certain parts of your concept.

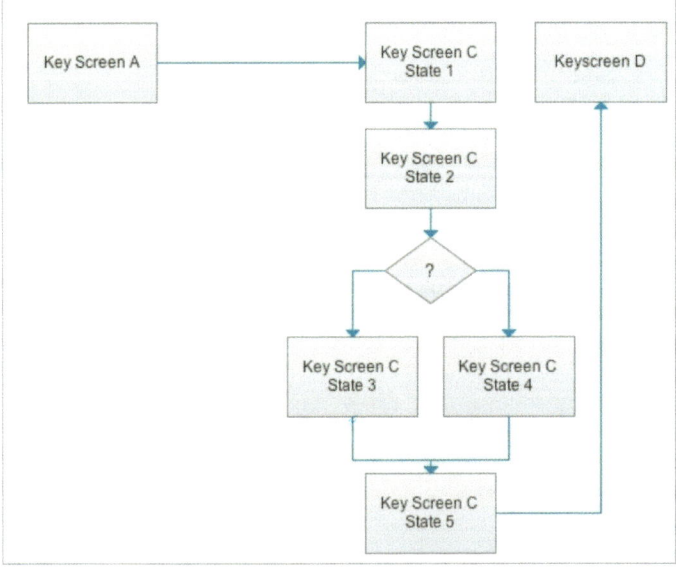

Interactivity

You can also prototype different levels of interactivity. You can start with user interface flows for selected use cases by turning them into a static 'slideshow', showing each screen of the flow. Later, you can refine these by making the screen's UI elements interactive and clickable. Last but not least, you can add animations and transitions to your prototype.

Visual Fidelity

You can apply different levels of visual fidelity to your prototype. Use hand-drawn sketches or the 'sketchy wireframe look' to communicate the draft status of your prototype. Or use Axure's standard UI elements and apply the look and feel of the mobile platform you are designing for, or you can even create you own visual design and use it in your prototype.

If you want to learn more about prototyping, I highly recommend the book by Todd Zaki Warfel called 'Prototyping' [216]. An important paper on the topic is 'What do Prototypes Prototype?' [217] by Stephanie Houde and Charles Hill.

Beware of Feature Creep!

The danger of using a sophisticated prototyping tool like Axure to get lost in its details and start to prototype something because it's an interesting or a fun problem to solve. (I know, because this happens to me all the time.) Feature creep doesn't only lurk in the programming environments of our peers, the developers, but also in our own tools.

Frequently question why you are doing something and whether the effort you are putting in gets you closer to achieve your prototype's goals. Compare your prototype with your product vision and your design tenets and stop as soon as your prototype is 'good enough' at answering your questions. You can always refine and improve it later.

What to Prototype

Let me share with you some rules I try to adhere to when prototyping:

- Always go for speed and quantity at the beginning.
- Create the big picture first (e.g. list all the key screens and their variants) and don't spend too much time on the nitty-gritty interaction details.
- Don't waste time polishing the look of your prototype; it is only a prototype after all.
- Never try to build the full solution in Axure (including all its variants and edge cases). It will only cause you grief. Seriously.
- Create prototypes for the more complex aspects of your solution, like interactions with multiple steps, new functionality and changes to the existing workflow.
- Prototype the most-used functionality – the Pareto Principle [239] offers a good rule of thumb: Prototype the 20% of the functionality that is going to be used 80% of the time. Another approach is to focus on what's critical (for a good UX) and complex (for the user).
- Stick to the important use cases. Explain the edge cases in writing (or with a diagram) – that's easier and faster.
- As Axure is quite powerful you will sometimes be tempted to create a 'hack' – that is a way to solve something that is not really supported by Axure but can be done. Evaluate beforehand how much complexity you want to introduce into your prototype. A hack will always increase your prototype's complexity.
- And the most important rule is: **good enough is really good enough**. Don't try to squeeze too much into your prototype. Complexity will fight back: maintaining and updating your prototype will take longer. Prototyping is a means, not an end in its own.

5. Setting up Axure

There are a couple of things needed to make your copy of Axure fully 'mobile ready': determine and set up your target screen resolution, fill in your prototype's mobile settings, enhance the CSS of your mobile prototype and get some free mobile libraries.

Defining Your Screen Estate

What is the right screen size for your prototype? Well, that depends on your targeted platform and the device you are prototyping for.

Pick Your Screen Resolution

Axure 7.0 offers two options for building prototypes. You can choose your target screen resolution beforehand and only focus on this resolution. Use this method if you don't want (or need) to show your prototype in different resolutions or on different devices. The more complex approach is to use Axure's 'Adaptive View' feature, which lets you create different layouts for different width and height values.

Regardless of your approach, however, you always need to determine the starting resolution for your prototype:

- For an **iPhone 3 or iPhone 4** prototype use 640x960px.
- For an **iPhone 5** one use 640x1136px.
- For an **iPad** prototype use 2048x1536px.
- On **Android, Windows Phone** and **Firefox OS** use the dimensions of the target device.

As you see above, I recommend using retina screen sizes for **iOS** prototypes, since I will show you how to scale down your prototype for non-retina screens, such as the iPhone 3. Your layouts will then look good on both retina and non-retina screens. If you create non-retina layouts instead, they will look blurry when viewed on retina screens. Scaling down allows you to design for retina and non-retina alike.

This approach will not work on **Android** and **Windows** since they offer different resolution classes with different scaling factors.

 Note: Building a prototype that works well on multiple operating systems (e.g. on both iOS and Android) is complicated, as their resolutions and aspect ratios don't match. Either focus on one platform i.e. one resolution at a time (my recommendation is to reduce efforts) or build an adaptive prototype covering both platforms.

Determine your Scaling Factor

The resolution you select also impacts the size of your UI elements. On **iOS** only two resolution categories exist: non-retina and retina. The later offers twice the screen height and width: The (non-retina) iPhone 3 has a resolution of 320x480px and the (retina) iPhone 4 has 640x960px. Even though the number of pixels increases on retina screens, the physical size of the display remains the same. Thus UI elements on a retina display are twice the size of a non-retina one, e.g. the status bar height is 20px for a non-retina screen and 40px for a retina one. Thus two scaling factors exists on iOS:

- non-retina = 1.0
- retina = 2.0.

On **Android**, things are a bit more complicated as it offers six resolution categories (LDPI, MDPI, HDPI, XHDPI – recently XXHDPI and XXXHDPI were added) with MDPI being the standard resolution.

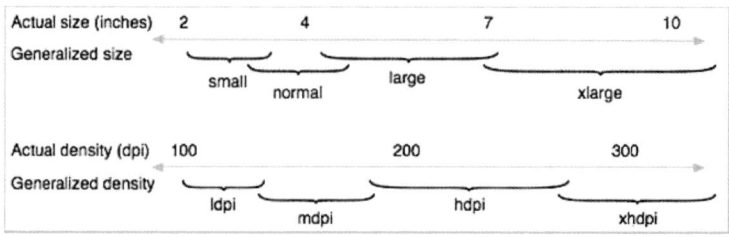

Depending on your targeted resolution category apply one of the following scaling factors to your UI elements' width and height values:

- LDPI = 0.75
- MDPI = 1.0
- HDPI = 1.5
- XHDPI = 2.0
- XXHDPI = 3.0
- XXXHDPI = 4.0.

An Android status bar is 20px in height in MDPI and 30px in the HDPI resolution (20px * 1.5 for HDPI).[1]

Windows Phone currently uses four resolution categories:

- 480x800px (WVGA)
- 1280x768px (WXGA)
- 1280x720px (HD720p)
- 1920x1080px (HD1080p).

Firefox OS does not differentiate any resolution categories. They recommend to build responsive apps (since it is an HTML-based operating system) instead. For an overview of the different Firefox OS screens sizes [253] take a look at Mozilla's device list.

Using Global Guides

After you selected your screen size and know your resolution category, set up your screen estate using *global guides*. Guides are helper lines you can drag on a page.

There are two types of guides: *global guides* that will be shown on all *pages*, and *page guides* that pertain only to a single *page*. *Global guides* are shown as pink lines in Axure, *page guides* are blue, and the currently active *guide* is green. When you drag UI elements around they can be docked onto your *guides*.

 Note: Axure 7.0 allows you to change the color used for *guides* (right-click on the canvas > Grid and Guides > Guide Settings).

Let me show you how to set up *global guides* using the dimensions of an font iPhone 4 (640x960px).

First, make *global guides* visible (right-click on the canvas > Grids and Guide > Show Global Guides. Or press CMD+'.' on a Mac or CMD +'.' on Windows).

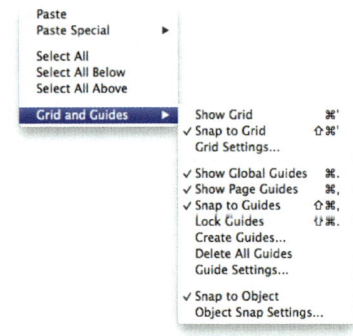

Next, drag a *global guide* from the horizontal ruler to 960px (hold CMD on a Mac or CTRL on Windows and drag).

Now, drag a *global guide* from the vertical ruler to 640px. The screen estate of your prototype is now defined.

You can add extra *guides* to delimit the landscape mode or to show the position of UI elements used in your prototype. I always add a *global guide* showing the height of the screen without the status bar (in this example: 920px = 960px - 40px status bar height). This *guide* gives me the effective height of my prototype since I usually layout my screens without the status bar.

The image below shows the canvas with *guides* for portrait and landscape mode and for the status bar.

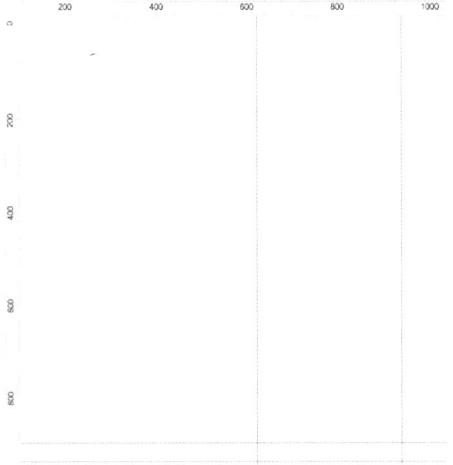

Note: You can right-click on a *guide* to lock it in its location or you can lock all guides (right-click > Grid and Guides > Lock Guides) at once.

Note: When you set up an *adaptive view* Axure will add a helper line that looks like a *global guide* (pink) for the width and/or height values you defined for as the view's breakpoint. This line cannot be dragged, deleted or hidden.

Using a Grid System

If you are creating a web app or a mobile website you might want to use a grid system to layout your screens. A grid system is a set of columns offering a framework to structure your screens' content. To create a grid system in Axure use the 'Create Guides' function (right-click on the canvas > Grids and Guide > Create Guides):

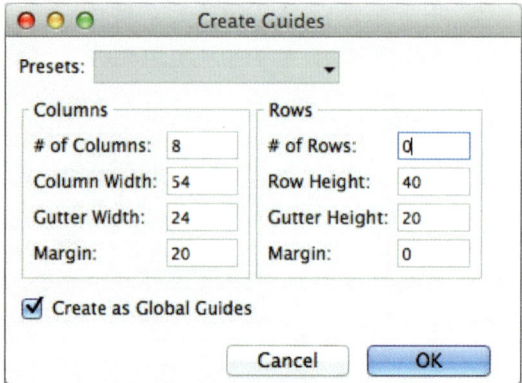

In the picture above I used the values of the mobile '300 Grid system' (adjusted for a iPhone 4) that is part of the 978.gs [141] grid system.

If you want to learn more about grid systems, please visit `thegridsystem.org` [143], take a look at the presentation from Khoi Vinh and Mark Boulton called 'Grids are Good' (.pdf – 9mb) [144] and read the articles 'Grid-based Web Design, simplified' [145] by Chris Brauckmuller and 'The Semantic Grid System' [146] by Tyler Tate.

Axure's Mobile Settings

To make sure that your prototype is properly displayed (and scaled) on your mobile device, you need to use Axure's mobile prototype settings. This is one the key elements (and one major hurdle) when building mobile prototypes with Axure.

Open 'Publish > Generate HTML Files' or press the F8 key on Windows or CMD+SHIFT+O on Mac and select the 'Mobile/Device' section.

 Note: These settings will also be applied when you upload your prototype to AxShare (see 'Using AxShare').

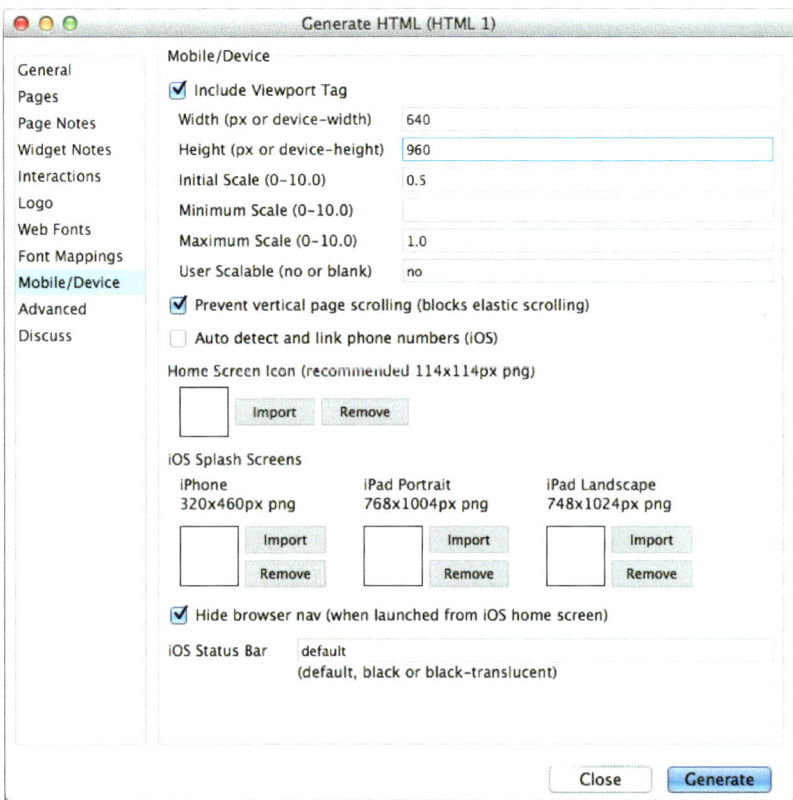

The Viewport Tag

First, check the 'Include Viewport Tag' checkbox.[2] Specify the resolution you are designing for. If you are unsure about the correct values, see the previous chapter.

	iPhone 3&4	iPhone 5	iPad	Android, Windows & Firefox	
Width	640	640	1536	device-width	[width]
Height	960	1136	2048		[height]
Initial Scale	0.5			1.0	1.0
Min. Scale					
Max. Scale	1.0			1.0	1.0
User Scalable	no, minimal-ui			no	no

For **iPhone 3 and iPhone 4** prototypes enter '640' in the width and '960' in the height field. To let non-retina iOS devices scale down your prototype, enter '0.5' in the 'Initial Scale' and '1.0' in the 'Maximum Scale' fields. Retina-displays will detect that they don't need to apply the scaling factor and will scale up. Now your prototype will look good on both retina and non-retina screens.

For an **iPhone 5** enter '640' and '1136' and set both 'Initial Scale' and 'Maximum Scale' to '1.0'.

Use the same logic for an **iPad** prototype and enter '1536' and '2048' as width and height values and '0.5' for 'Initial Scale' and 1.0 for 'Maximum Scale'.

 Note: Using the larger resolution will increase the size of your prototype – especially when you use a lot of graphics in it.

For **Android, Windows Phone and Firefox OS** you need to enter 'device-width' in the width field instead of providing pixel values. If you do, keep the height field empty. Set the 'Initial Scale' and 'Maximum Scale' to '1.0'. Alternatively, you can hardcode the width and height values. You can use the page created by Ryan Van Etten to determine the viewport settings [226] of your device.

Last but not least, set 'User Scalable' to 'no'. This sets the zoom level to the original size and disables zooming.

 Note: With **iOS 7.1** a new viewport meta tag was introduced: 'minimal-ui'. It triggers a full-screen mode when set. You no longer need to save your prototype as a web app to get a full-screen view. Set the tag in Axure by adding it to the 'User Scalable' field: 'no, minimal-ui'. For more information see Maximilliano Flirtman's article on the topic [250].

Note: On **Android**, some browsers (e.g. Chrome) will override your viewport settings. If you get unexpected results, try another browser. My recommendation is the 'Kiosk Browser' by Andy Powell.

Vertical Scrolling
Depending on how you are going to implement scrolling in your prototype (see the 'Scrolling' chapter), you need to check or uncheck the 'Prevent vertical page scrolling' checkbox. Uncheck it for now.

Auto-detect phone numbers (iOS)
Uncheck the 'Auto-detect and link phone numbers' checkbox since this function only interferes with your prototype's content.

Splash Screens
Don't use this option. Creating a splash screen within your prototype offers you more possibilities – plus it works on all mobile operating systems. See the 'Splash Screen' chapter for more information.

iOS Browser Navigation
Set this option when you want to place a shortcut to your prototype on your home screen. See the 'Creating a Web App' chapter for more details.

iOS Status Bar Behavior
You can also define the color of the iOS status bar. This setting will affect how your prototype will be displayed:

- A **'black-translucent' status bar will overlay the prototype** (your prototype will be positioned at (0, 0) but your content needs to start at (0, 40). Using the 'black-translucent' setting on iOS7 will give you white text and a fully transparent background.
- The other two options (**'default' or 'black') will place the status bar above your prototype** (your prototype will start at (0, 40)).

No sitemap

Last but not least, go back to the 'General' section of the 'Generate HTML' dialog and select the 'Without Sitemap' option. Now your prototype will be shown without the sidebar on the left-hand side.

 Note: This setting does not work with prototypes hosted on AxShare. But you can define a default page for your prototype (thus removing the sitemap) in the 'Pretty URLs' section on share.axure.com.

Improving Axure's CSS

Even though Axure 7.0 includes several settings to make your prototype mobile-friendly, there are some additional CSS statements that will further improve your prototype:

```
* {
    outline: none;
    -webkit-text-size-adjust: none;
    -webkit-touch-callout: none;
    -webkit-user-select: none;
}
input, textarea {
    -webkit-user-select: auto;
}
```

The first line disables the highlight for UI elements. The second tells the browser not to scale the displayed text. The third line disables the callout overlay you get when you long-press a link, and the fourth line disables the 'copy and paste' popover. The last two lines re-enable it for input fields, to keep them selectable.

To make your (and my) life easier, I built a *master* that will automatically insert the above CSS code to the current *page* of your prototype. You can find it in the book's source files.

Free Mobile Resources

You are not the first person building a mobile prototype and this is a good thing, because it means there are already plenty of mobile resources available to make your life easier. You'll find a list of freely available Axure libraries, UI element and icon collections on the books' website.

---

[1] For more information about the UI element sizes of the different mobile platforms look at iPhone [065], Android [066] and Windows Phone-specific information [067]. For an overview of the different screen resolutions [068] see this article by David Storey.

[2] David Calhoun provides an excellent overview over viewport meta tag options [069].

6. Building Mobile Prototypes

When building a prototype, *pages* and *dynamic panels* are your main building blocks. *Pages* usually contain the different screens of your prototype, while *dynamic panels* allow you to define interactive areas, e.g. an initially empty list which gets populated or parts of a screen where a dialog box will be shown.

You usually use *pages* to store your prototype's screens. A *page*-based prototype is a set of *pages* linked together. This is the typical way to build website prototypes. But you can also use *dynamic panels* to store the screens of your prototype. A *panel-based* prototype (usually) features a single *dynamic panel* containing your prototype's screens. Instead of linking pages you toggle the *panel states* of the *dynamic panel*. This means you'll use the 'Widget Manager' instead of the 'Sitemap' section to keep track of your prototype's screens. This approach is useful when prototyping mobile apps.

But choosing the right approach depends on several factors:

- **Complexity**: It is very easy to create a couple of *pages* and link them together. Building *panel*-based prototypes takes a bit more time and practice.
- **Transitions**: There are no *page* transitions in Axure, only *panels* can feature transitions. To show transitions between screens you need to create a *panel*-based prototypes.
- **Animations**: You can only prototype animations with *dynamic panels*.
- **Navigation**: You can only use the browser's navigation buttons in *page*-based prototypes. The 'back' button will not navigate between *panel* states.
- **Gestures**: Only *dynamic panels* allow you to detect swiping gestures.

- **Loading Time**: A short delay will occur every time a new *page* is loaded. Thus *page*-based prototypes offers a realistic web browsing experience. A *panel*-based prototype will be fully loaded when it is first opened because it consists of a single *page*. Thus *panel*-based prototypes are better suited to showcase an app's behavior.
- **Specifications**: Creating a specification is much easier for *page*-based prototypes. It can also be done for *panel*-based ones, as I explain in the 'Creating Documentation' chapter, but it needs a few additional steps.
- **Element reuse**: When using *pages* you will store reoccurring elements (your page header, tabs, etc.) as *masters*. For a *panel*-based prototype you need to use a different approach. Turn your prototype's content area into a *dynamic panel* (e.g. the space below the header and above a tab bar) and create the static elements only once.

Generally speaking, a *page*-based approach is better suited for mobile websites and low-fidelity app prototypes. Use this method if you need results fast or if you want to present a basic concept.

A *panel*-based approach is better suited for apps and high-fidelity prototypes. It offers more interaction possibilities (swiping gestures, animations and transitions) and provides a structure that allows you to gradually increase its fidelity. But it is a bit harder to build and maintain. But this is not a 'black or white' choice you need to make. You will find yourself mixing both approaches depending on the project at hand.

Page-based Prototypes

The simplest way to build a prototype in Axure is to link different *pages* together. First, create a *page* for each key screen your solution will have. If you need to show a screen in different states (e.g. first an empty form, then a filled form), create sub-pages for each one. I usually put the name of the state in brackets.

Next, you want to add some content and interactive elements to your *pages*. You could start with scribbles or full screen images created in Photoshop (or in a similar tool). Add hotspots to make parts of your screens clickable.

Alternatively, use the elements of Axure's default 'Wireframe' widget library or use custom-made ones to layout your screens. Use the *events* the elements provide to make your prototype interactive. The simplest option is to use the 'OnClick' *event* to connect your screens.

Panel-based Prototypes

This approach uses a single *dynamic panel* to store all the screen of your prototype. First, create a *dynamic panel* on your 'Home' *page* with *states* for each (key) screen. Resize it to match it to your screen resolution (e.g. 640x920px – without the status bar) and position it in the top-left corner (0, 0) of your page. Last but not least, give it a decent name (e.g. 'prototype').

Next, you want to create *dynamic panels* to collect the various states of the individual screens. Open the *panel state* corresponding to a screen and add a new *dynamic panel*. Create a *state* for each screen variant. Below, I added an extra *panel* for the 'login' screen.

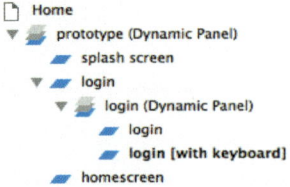

Don't forget to resize, position and label the *panel* and its *states* accordingly. The diagram below shows the structure of a typical *panel-*based prototype:

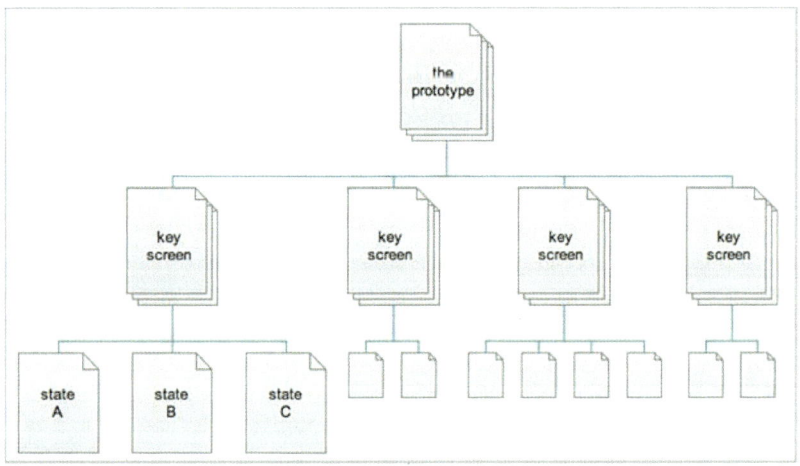

Differences to a Page-based Prototype

Since all your prototype screens exist within a *dynamic panel* you cannot use the 'OnPageLoad' *event* to initialize your prototype's screens. Use the 'OnLoad' *event* (for initializing) or the 'OnPanelStateChange' event (to load information for specific screens) of the main *dynamic panel* instead. When you use the 'OnPanelStateChange' *event* you have to add a *condition* to check for the correct *panel state* because this *event* is called every time the *panel's state* changes.

In the example below (taken from the 'Splash Screens' chapter) I use the 'OnPanelStateChange' *event* to animate the splash screen of an app:

```
▼ ᵗ⅓ OnPanelStateChange
  ▼ 🖥 slpash?
       (If state of panel overview equals splash screen)
     ⚡ Wait 1500 ms
     ⚡ Show loadingIndicator
     ⚡ Wait 3500 ms
     ⚡ Hide loadingIndicator
     ⚡ Set overview state to content
```

And as mentioned before, the 'Back' button will not work (it will open the previous page stored in your browser history) since your prototype consists of a single *page*.

Structuring Your Prototype

Let me share with you some best practices for structuring your prototype. Start by asking yourself the following questions to determine the structure of your prototype:

- What is the most common layout of your screens? How many different types of screens does your prototype contain?
- What are static elements of your prototype – e.g. tabs, a global navigation or headers? In a *page*-based prototype are these usually candidates for *masters*. A *page*-based prototype will be heavier on *masters*, since you want to reuse the static elements for the different screens. In a *panel*-based prototype these elements are often implemented as *dynamic panels*.
- What are dynamic elements of your prototype – like lists or popups? These will be built via *dynamic panels*.

The better you structure your prototype, the better you'll remember what you did when you reopen it after some time. It also makes it easier for others to 'get' what you did.

Start by creating *pages*, *masters* and *dynamic panels* for your prototype. Focus solely on the structure and add *interactions* later. Label all your *panels*, *cases* and key elements. And your prototypes should not need more than three levels of *dynamic panels* – remember how confusing the movie 'Inception' became once they entered the third (dream) layer.

Web Prototypes

The following example will show you how to build a typical mobile website prototype. A website usually contains a page header that spans across the full page, containing a logo and the page's title, with the main navigation and the site content below.

The header, the logo and tab bar are good candidates for *masters*. The content below is centered with some padding to the left and right, creating a 'safe area'.

In the example above I used a 40px padding on both sides, resulting in a 560px (= 640px - 80px) safe area on an iPhone. Create two *global guides* to delimit the safe area.

To tell Axure to center your *page's* content, click on the 'Page Style' tab and set the 'Page Align' to centered. You can also set a background color for your *page*.

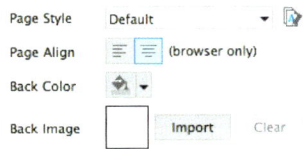

Page Style	Default ▾
Page Align	⯈ ⯈ (browser only)
Back Color	🔸 ▾
Back Image	☐ Import Clear

ⓘ **Note:** The easiest way to apply these settings to all your prototype's *pages* is to create a custom 'Page Style' and assign it to your *pages*. Click on the icon next to the 'Page Style' dropdown to define one.

To highlight the web safe area, add a *rectangle* to the *page* that matches the width of your safe area, give it a different color and use the 'lock' icon in Axure's toolbar to place it in the background and lock its position.

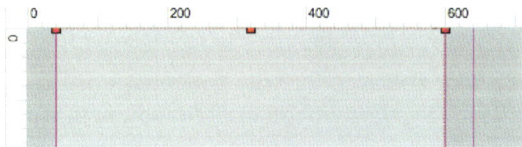

Next, build the page header. Add a *dynamic panel* to your *page* and label it 'header'. Place it at (0, 0) and give it a decent height (e.g. 120px) and the width of your target resolution (640px).

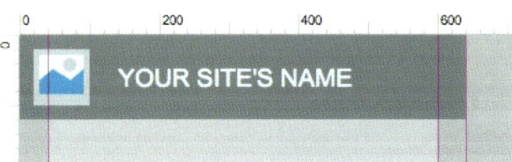

Double-click on it to open it's only *state*. Add an *image widget* as a placeholder for the page logo and a *label* for the page title. Assign a background color to the *panel state* (a new feature of Axure 7.0) in the 'Panel State Formatting' tab as well. Close the *panel state* and you are done.

Note: If you want to keep the header on top when scrolling your *page*, click on the 'Pin to browser' link and choose 'Keep in front' and 'top-left' in the 'Panel Properties'.

You can also tell Axure to expand the banner across the full *page*, also a new feature of Axure 7.0. If you now rotate your phone or view the prototype on a larger screen, your header will still span across the full *page* while your content remains centered and on top. If you want to find out how to make your prototype fully responsive, check out the 'Adaptive Views' chapter.
Close the *panel* and check the '100% Wide' checkbox.

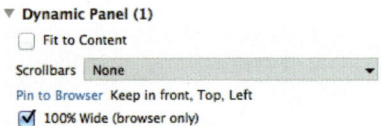

Last but not least, turn the header into a *master* since you will use it on all your *pages*. Now you can start adding the main navigation (e.g. a tab bar) and fill your *page* with content.

App Prototypes
An app prototype is usually structured differently. Let's discuss the screenshot below. The screen consists of a static header, a content area with three pages and a paging indicator on the bottom of the screen.

All three elements (header, content section and the paging indicator) are candidates for *dynamic panels*. The header and the paging indicator are static – in terms of placement. You want to update their content when the main area's content changes. Tie swiping actions to the main content *panel* and use its 'OnPanelStateChange' *event* to update the other two *dynamic panels*.

- OnClick
- ▼ OnPanelStateChange
  - ▼ update header & indicator
    - Set value of currentPage equal to state of This
    - Set page indicator to [[currentPage]]
    - Set header to [[currentPage]]
- OnDragStart
- OnDrag
- OnDragDrop
- ▼ OnSwipeLeft
  - ▼ Case 1
    - Set This to Next slide left out 500ms slide left in 500ms
- ▼ OnSwipeRight
  - ▼ Case 1
    - Set This to Previous slide right out 500ms slide right in 500ms

For more information on how to build this screen, check out the 'Swiping' chapter.

7. Viewing your Prototype

While working on your prototype you want to check frequently what parts of it work and what parts can be improved.

To view your prototype, press the 'Preview' button (or the F6 key on Windows or CMD+SHIFT+P on a Mac). The prototype's HTML files will be generated on-the-fly (a new feature of Axure 7.0) and your prototype will be opened in your browser. You no longer need to re-generate your prototype after every update. Use the browser's refresh button to see the changes you made.

You still have the option to create all HTML files (F8 on Windows or CMD+SHIFT+O on a Mac), e.g. if you want to copy them to a mobile device or email them to other people.

 Note: Axure will open the browser you defined in the 'Generate HTML' dialog (F8 on Windows or CMD+SHIFT+O on a Mac) and will apply the settings you defined there.

You have several options for showcasing your prototype:
- access it from an online source
- store it on your mobile
- mirror the prototype from your computer
- show it on a large screen
- use a mobile simulator
- build a native mobile app.

Details on Viewing

But before I walk you through the different options, I briefly want to explain how to get the URL of your prototype, how the viewing options impact the display of the status bar, how you'll be able to show your prototypes in full-screen mode and to lock the device rotation.

Getting Your Prototype's URL

If your prototype opens with the sidebar visible, you want to get the URL of the real page and get rid of the sidebar.

Open your prototype's start page and click on the chain link icon. Select the 'without site map' radio button and copy the link. This is the link to your prototype's HTML page. Or click the 'x' to close the sidebar – then the active page will be reloaded without the sidebar.

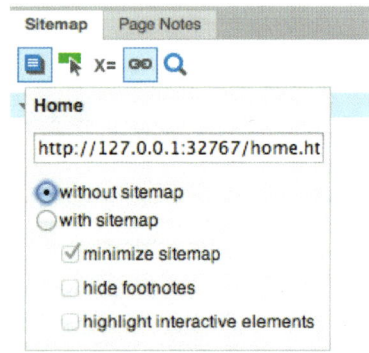

 Note: In the picture above you can see that I am using the URL from a prototype created via Axure's 'Preview' function (it uses the localhost IP address: 127.0.0.1). In most cases you will want to put your prototype online or store its HTML files on your device. But you can use the on-the-fly prototype with a mobile simulator.

Using QR Codes

One (obvious) way to view your prototype on your mobile device is to open the browser and type in the address of your prototype – but this is quite cumbersome. A more convenient way is to create a QR code of the URL and read it with your mobile device. This frees you from typing the URL on your mobile's (tiny) virtual keyboard.

The easiest way to create a QR code is to use the bookmarklet [168] by Faisal Iqbal. After adding it to your browser's bookmark bar you can click it to display a QR code with the URL of the current web page. Or you can use an online service like 'kaywa' or an application (e.g. 'QREncoder' for Mac).

To read the QR code on your mobile device you need to install a QR reader app (e.g. 'Scan' [169], 'QR Droid' [170] for Android or 'i-nigma' for Windows Phone). Snap a picture of the QR code, let the app decode it and view your prototype in your mobile browser.

Your Phone's Status Bar

If you are showing your prototype on a mobile phone, the operating system's status bar (the one showing the time and the battery icon) may be placed above your prototype or shown on top as an overlay – or it might not be shown at all. This depends on your OS and on the browser or the app you use to view your prototype.

That's why I recommend **designing the screens of your prototype without the status bar.** Reduce the height of your prototype by the status bar height.

 Note: On iOS 7 Safari no longer shows the status bar in landscape mode. Use the full height of your screen.

Full-Screen Mode

You have several options to view your HTML prototype full-screen. On **Firefox** and **Android** you can use the JavaScript Fullscreen API. Add 'screenful.js' [254] (a Fullscreen API wrapper) to your prototype's HTML. (For details on how to change your prototype's HTML see the 'Advanced Topics' chapter.)

On **Android** most alternative browsers (e.g. 'Dolphin', 'Mercury') offer a full-screen viewing mode.

On **iOS** you can create a web app (see the next section) or you can use the 'minimal-ui' viewport meta tag (see 'Setting up Axure'). And most iOS offline viewers offer a full-screen viewing mode as well.

Creating a Web App (on iOS)

To see the options you defined in the mobile settings in action (splash screen and app icon definition, and status bar behavior) you need to create a 'web app' – which is Apple lingo for: create a link to the prototype on your device's home screen.

First, check the 'Hide browser nav' checkbox in Axure's mobile settings (Publish > Generate HTML Files > Mobile/Device). Then, put your prototype online and view it in Safari. Click the 'Action' button (the one with the arrow) and select 'Add to Home Screen'.

If you specified an app icon you will see it now (otherwise you'll see a thumbnail of your prototype) and you'll be asked to name your web app. Afterwards, the web app is added to your home screen.

Disable Auto-Rotation

If you don't plan to build a responsive prototype (see 'Adaptive Views'), it's a good idea to disable the auto-rotation feature of your device. Otherwise the screen orientation might change accidentally while you show your prototype and mess up your presentation.

On **iOS**, swipe up to show the 'Control Center'. The top-right button allows you to lock the screen. On the iPhone this will lock the phone in portrait mode, on an iPad the current orientation will be locked.

On **Android** the function could be in your phone's settings (Settings > Display) or an option in the notification menu, depending on your phone's vendor. But there are also quite a few widgets available in the Google Play store [166] that allow you to lock the orientation.

On **Windows Phone** you can disable the auto-rotation feature in the settings (Settings > Screen Rotation).

Unfortunately **Firefox OS** does not offer this possibility (yet).

Online Prototypes

You can use third party services like 'AxShare' or 'Dropbox' to put your prototype online. But before you choose this option consider whether you (or your company) are comfortable storing your prototype on external servers.

Using AxShare

The easiest way to put your prototype online is to use AxShare, Axure's built prototype-sharing platform. If you hit the 'AxShare' button (F6 on Windows or CMD+SHIFT+A on Mac) or use 'Publish > Publish to AxShare' you will get a popup asking you for your AxShare credentials. If you don't have any (yet) you can sign up for free.

When you use AxShare your source (.rp) file will be uploaded to Axure's server and the HTML output will be created there. You can specify a password (with at least four characters) you'll have to enter when opening the prototype.

 Note: AxShare's password dialog is currently not mobile-friendly. But you can make a mobile-friendly login dialog part of your prototype.

On the AxShare website you can define the starting page for your prototype and its (404) error page. You can also add custom HTML, CSS and JavaScript code to your online prototype.

Pros and Cons:
+   AxShare is tightly integrated into Axure
+   You can specify an access password
−   Your prototype's source file gets uploaded to an external server

Using Dropbox

Another easy way to get your prototype online is to use 'Dropbox', a cloud service. Dropbox allows you to host your prototype's HTML code online and share the URL to your prototype.

Copy the folder containing your prototype's HTML code into your Dropbox. Select the 'index.html' (or the starting page of your prototype) in your Finder (on a Mac) or your File Explorer (on Windows) and get the URL (right click > Copy public link) to access your prototype.

Pros and Cons:

+   You only need to copy your prototype to your Dropbox folder
+   No (applicable) size restrictions
−   No password control − anyone can access it
−   Your prototype's HTML files are uploaded to an external server

Using Your Own Web Space

This is a variation of the Dropbox procedure: Copy the HTML output to your own web server, get the URL and view your prototype. (I am assuming that if you own web space you already know how to get stuff online, so I won't describe it here.)

Pros and Cons:

+   Full control over access rights
−   For advanced users only

Prototypes on Your Mobile

You can also store your prototype's HTML files on your mobile. This way you don't have to rely on an internet connection when viewing it. Your prototype will be faster since the HTML files are stored locally.

On **iOS** you can use offline HTML viewers like 'Sites-2-Go' or 'ProtoSee'. To upload your prototype you can use iTunes (drop a .zip archive into its storage in the apps tab) or a web interface (both apps can start a local web server on your device to provide you an upload form). Once you have uploaded your .zip archive you can view its content.

 Note: To activate full-screen mode in Sites-2-Go tap inside the content window and shake your iOS device once.

On **Android** you can copy your prototype's HTML files onto your device's SD card (or to its internal storage). To 'find' the files you need to use an Android file explorer, e.g. the 'ES File Explorer'. Use it to open your prototype in your mobile browser. A good full screen browser for Android is the 'Kiosk Browser'. On **Windows Phone** you can use an app called 'Offline Browser'. For **Firefox OS** see the 'Creating a Native App' chapter, since uploading a prototype to a Firefox device turns it into a native app.

Pros and Cons:

+ Works without a network connection
+ Fast, since files don't need to be downloaded
− You need to re-upload your prototype after each change

Mirror Your Prototype

You can also choose to mirror your prototype from your computer to your mobile. You can use 'Adobe Edge Inspect CC' or 'Ghostlab'. The advantage of these tools is that they send the HTML code of your prototype to your mobile.

The second best option is to use a mirror application (e.g. 'Reflector' or 'iScreen') that allows you to show your phone's screen on your computer. Other mirroring solutions (e.g. 'xScopeMirror', 'LiveView' or the 'Android Design Preview') work the other way around – they display a part of your computer screen on a mobile.

Pros and Cons:
+ Easy to install and run
+ Works on Android and iOS
− Mirroring apps are usually paid software

Showing Prototypes on a Larger Screen

If you showcase your prototype on a larger screen (on a pad, a computer screen or a projector) it's best to place it 'inside' a device screenshot. This allows you to check how your prototype's UI will look on a smaller screen. Otherwise, your UI elements might be too small or your screens will be too crowded. Plus it gives your prototype a more realistic look.

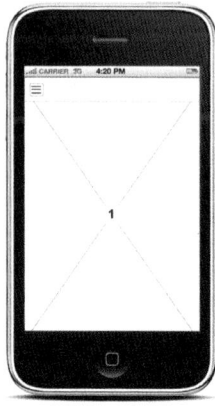

You can add a short description next to your prototype describing the supported use cases, the key take-aways or add topics for discussion. And don't forget to center your prototype (Page Style > Page Align) – it looks nicer.

Pros and Cons:

+ Good for presentation and discussions
− Not the 'real thing' – it's always better to view your prototype on a real mobile device

Using a Mobile Simulator

If you want to test your prototype but you don't have a mobile device at hand you can view your prototype via a mobile simulator.

 Note: Since I don't own a Windows PC I was only able to test the iOS, Android and Firefox simulators.

iOS Simulator

Install 'XCode' on your Mac via the App Store. Locate the iOS simulator [175] and open it. Once it is up and running you'll see an iPhone. (Unfortunately Apple removed the surrounding device image with OS 10.9, Mavericks.)

You can change the device type (iPhone/iPad) and the orientation of the device (CMD+'Cursor left' or CMD+'Cursor right'). You can open local and online URLs and copy and paste URLs into Safari. If you saved your prototype as a web app, the simulator will keep the app on the home screen. Even after you close (and reopen) the simulator.

Pros and Cons:
+   Easy to install and to use
+   Supports local URLs
+   Allows you to copy and paste URLs

 Note: You can use the 'SimFinger' [179] plugin to add app icons of pre-installed apps to the emulator. It also allows you to replace your cursor with a finger (thus the name). Loren Brichter describes the plugin in more detail in his blog. (Since his site is no longer online I used the Wayback Machine's stored copy [180] to access it.)

Android Emulator

To be frank: the Android emulator is less fun than the iOS one. Only use it if you have to. Seriously.

First, downloading [176] and installing it [177] is not easy. You need to work with the command line quite a bit to get it up and running. You cannot paste URLs into its browser. The easiest way to get them into the emulator is to send them via SMS [178] from the command line. And it won't accept local URLs (`file://`). And it's not a beauty – but if you are into it, you can decide to skin it [235].

Pros and Cons:

—   Hard to install, only for advanced users

—   No local URL support

Firefox OS Simulator

The newest kid on the block is the Firefox OS simulator. It is the easiest one to install since it is a Firefox browser plugin [236]. Once you have it installed you can start the emulator from the 'Tool > Web Developer' menu.

You can open local files and it's easy to turn your prototype's HTML files into an app (see the next chapter).

Pros and Cons:
+   Easy to install and to use
+   Allows you to copy and paste URLs
+   Supports local URLs

Creating a Native App

If you want to turn your prototype into a native app for **Android** or **Windows Phone** you can use PhoneGap Build [231], an online service by Adobe. Barbara Ballard explained how to use it [232] in the Axure forum. You can also use PhoneGap to create an **iOS** app, but for this you need to be part of the iOS developer program and it takes a few additional steps, like creating and importing key files. Martin Thiemann has written a German tutorial [233] on how to use PhoneGap with iOS. To create a **Firefox OS** app you simply need to zip your prototype and add a 'manifest.webapp' [234] file to the archive. Here is a sample manifest file:

```
{
  "name": "Axure Test App",
  "description": "My elevator pitch goes here",
  "launch_path": "/home.html",
  "fullscreen": "true",
  "icons": {
  "128": "/img/icon-128.png"
  },
  "developer": {
  "name": "YourNameHere",
  "url": "http://your-homepage-here.org"
  },
  "default_locale": "en"
}
```

Add the archive via the Firefox Simulator to your phone (or to the simulator). If you want to find out more about Firefox web apps, check out the Firefox OS Boilerplate App [237] project.

If you want to find out more about building mobile apps, take look at the series of articles by Peter Traeg [247] at Smashing Magazine.

8. Prototyping Interactions

This chapter will teach you which *events* in Axure are useful for building mobile prototypes, how to create animations and transitions and how to prototype basic behavior such as scrolling and swiping.

Events for Mobile

With Axure you are no longer restricted to static wireframes and key screens. Axure allows you to create interactive prototypes to showcase the targeted experience of your product. To create interactive prototypes you have to use Axure's *events* and *actions*. *Events* allow you to detect interactive behavior within your prototypes. With *actions* you can manipulate your prototypes' UI elements and screens.

There are *events* to determine user actions (like tapping and swiping) and *events* to track the behavior of Axure's UI elements (e.g. does a *panel state* change?). But not all of Axure's user behavior *events* are needed for mobile prototyping. The table below lists the user *actions* and the corresponding *events* applicable for mobile.

 Note: You cannot use pinch and other multi-touch gestures since your prototypes are HTML-based. These gestures are handled by the browser, e.g. zooming the page in or out.

User Action	Axure Event	Available
Tap	OnClick	All
Double Tap	OnDoubleClick	All
Press	OnMouseDown (OnMouseUp)	All
Long Press	OnLongClick	All
Swiping	OnSwipeLeft OnSwipeRight OnSwipeUp OnSwipeDown	Panels
Drag & Drop	OnDragStart OnDrag OnDragDrop	Panels
Scrolling	OnScroll OnPageScroll	Panels Pages
Typing	OnKeyDown (OnKeyUp)	Text Fields Text Areas
Rotates the phone	OnWindowResize OnAdaptiveViewChange	Pages

As you'll see in the 'Mobile UI Patterns' chapter, 'Show', 'Hide', 'OnLoad', 'OnWindowLoad', 'OnMove', 'OnPanelStateChange', 'OnFocus' and 'OnLostFocus' are *events* that you'll use frequently to track your prototype's behavior.

Animations and Transitions

Another key element of well-designed mobile apps and websites is good use of animations and transitions. They provide a sense of direction and help users orient themselves within your app. For some great examples, take a look at the following iOS apps: 'Reeder', 'Tweetbot', 'Flipboard', 'Path' or 'Sparrow'. The Windows Phone User Interface also uses a lot of subtle animations and transitions [155].

If you want to learn more about animations and transitions visit 'www.ui-transitions.com' [034], the articles 'Storyboarding iPad Transitions' [036] by Greg Nudelman, 'Mission Transition' [035] from Mark Cossey and the article 'A New Mobile Design Material' [156] by Rachel Hinman. Another good article is 'Great Animations Make Great Apps' [157] by Ben Johnson, in which he categorizes animations by their purpose.

Animations and Transitions in Axure

With Axure 6.5 you were only able to animate *dynamic panels*. Version 7.0 allows you to tie animations to any element. Use the following *actions* to animate content:

- The '**Move**', '**Scroll to Widget**' and '**Set Panel Size**' *actions* allow you to define an element's movements (swing, linear, ease in and/ or out, bounce or elastic).
- The *dynamic panel's* '**OnDrag**' *event* allows you define (which and) how an element will be moved via the drag action.
- The '**Hide**', '**Show**' and '**Set Panel State**' *actions* allow you to define how elements appear or disappear from view. You can fade content in (or out) and slide it in (or out) of view.

To see the different animations and transitions in action, take a look at this Axure prototype [238].

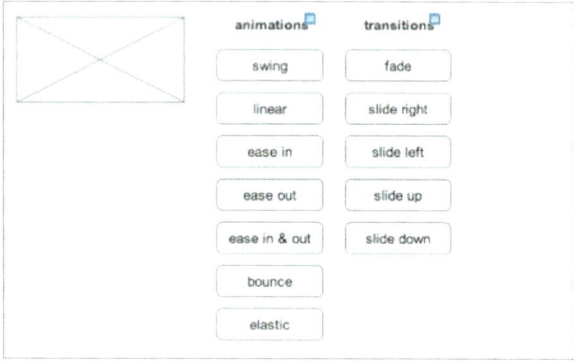

Unfortunately Axure does not allow you to define *page* transitions e.g. for the 'Open Link in' *action*. To prototype *page* transitions you need to put your screens inside a *dynamic panel* and use the 'Set Panel State' *action*. For more details see the 'Building Mobile Prototypes' chapter.

In the 'Mobile UI Patterns' chapter you will find various patterns that use fading ('Dialogs and Popups'), sliding ('Accordion Lists', Fullscreen on Scroll', 'Swiping', 'Sliding Menus') and movement ('Sliding Menus', 'Drag to Refresh') animations and transitions.

Prototyping Basic Behavior

In this section you'll see how to prototype basic behavior such as scrolling and swiping, and how to assign UI elements to a fixed position.

Scrolling

Pages and *dynamic panels* can contain scrollable content. You can either rely on the browser-based scrolling (by placing content outside the viewport) for both *pages* and *panels,* or you can manually enable scrollbars on *dynamic panels*. Use browser-based scrolling in your prototypes. Only choose *panel*-based scrolling for app prototypes that have fixed UI elements (like headers and tab bars above and/or below your content *panel*).

Scrolling On Pages

Making a *page* scrollable in Axure is fairly easy: if its content is outside the viewport (or larger than the viewport) scrollbars will be shown in the browser. To enable browser-based scrolling you need to uncheck the 'Prevent vertical page scrolling' checkbox in the Mobile/Device Settings (see 'Axure's Mobile Settings').

If you want to place static elements (e.g. a header or a tab bar) on a scrollable *page* you need to use the 'Pin to browser' functionality described in the 'Static Positioning' chapter.

Scrolling Inside Dynamic Panels

With Axure 7.0 you can use the same mechanism with *dynamic panels*.

Axure introduced a 'Fit to Content' checkbox in the 'Widget Properties' that allows you to create a similar effect. If you check it, the *panel* will adjust its size to the content of the currently active *panel state*. If its content is larger than your current viewport, you'll be able to scroll.

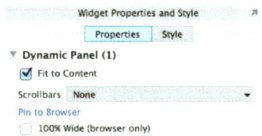

The *dynamic panel's* width and height will be based on the active *panel state's* content and it will be resized every time the *panel state* changes.

 Note: This also means that an empty *panel state* results in a tiny, almost invisible *dynamic panel*. Switching to an empty *state* will resize your *panel* to 10x10px.

Alternatively you can tell Axure to add scrollbars to your *dynamic panel*, while retaining its size. Use this if you need to create a 'fixed' layout (e.g., a static header and a *panel* with dynamic content below it) .

To enable scrolling for a *panel* right-click on it (or use the 'Widget Properties and Style' tab) and select: 'Show Scrollbars as needed'. If you have multiple levels of *dynamic panels* you need to enable scrolling on the main *dynamic panel* and on all sub-*panels*.

After activation the *panel* will show the bulky web scrollbars in Axure, but in your prototype they will be replaced with the (small) native scrollbars of your mobile platform.

Last but not least, check the 'Prevent vertical page scrolling' checkbox in the 'Mobile/Device Settings' because the scrollable content is now contained inside the *dynamic panel* (see 'Axure's Mobile Settings').

Working With Scrolling Events
To see how to use the new scrolling *events* and *variables* of Axure 7.0, take a look at the 'Fullscreen on Scroll' and the 'Sticky Headers for Lists' chapters.

Swiping

Axure offers *events* to detect vertical and horizontal swiping gestures performed on *dynamic panels*. Let's say you have three screens you want to be able to swipe through. Put your screens in a single *dynamic panel*.

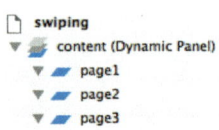

Click on the *dynamic panel* and take a look at the 'Interactions' tab. You should see something like this:

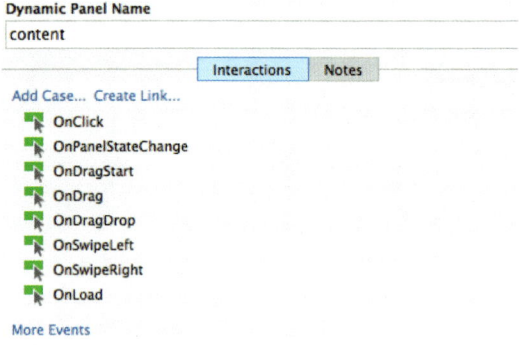

The 'OnSwipeLeft' and 'OnSwipeRight' *events* are already part of the list. The vertical ones are hidden behind the 'More Events' link. Double-click the 'OnSwipeLeft' *event* to define your first *case*. Select the 'Set Panel State' on 'This Widget' and don't select a particular *state*, use the 'Next' option instead. Set the 'Wrap from last to first' checkbox for 'infinite swiping'.

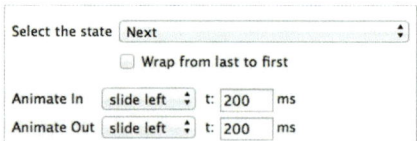

If you preview your prototype, you'll be able to swipe left but there is no sliding transition shown yet. Use the 'Animate In' and 'Animate Out' options of the 'SetPanelState' *action* to create one. Set both to 'slide left' to create a proper swiping transition. Repeat this for the 'OnSwipeRight' *event* using the 'Previous' *action*:

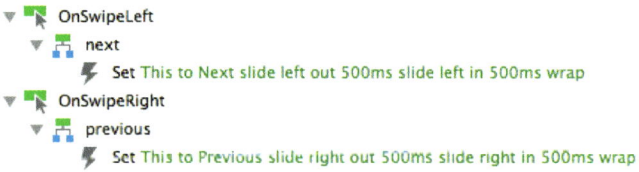

Now you are able to swipe back and forth.

Swiping and Element Placement

In the previous chapter I walked you through a simple example, showing how to swipe from one screen to the next. But often you have screens with fixed and dynamic UI elements that need to be built differently.

Let's prototype a slightly more complex screen, consisting of a fixed header , a page indicator and three screens.

Reuse the *dynamic panel* content of the previous example but reduce the *panel* height by 100 pixels to make room for the header. Move the content *panel* down by 100 pixels and place a *rectangle* (that's your header) on top. Copy it, you'll reuse it in a second, and turn it into a *dynamic panel* (right-click > Convert to Dynamic Panel). Add two more *states* to it (it will contain one header for each screen) and paste in each *state* the *rectangle*. Update its title.

Now label the header *panel* (e.g. 'header') and its *states*. It's important that you label the *states* of both *panels* the same. This will make changing their *states* easier. The resulting structure should look like this:

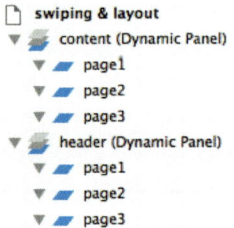

Next, drag a *placeholder* on you *page* and click the grey bubble in the top-right corner to change it to a circle. Resize it to 20x20px and you have created your first paging indicator. Copy and paste it twice and change the color of the first one. Move them to the bottom of your page. Copy the three elements and turn them into a *dynamic panel* (right-click > Convert to Dynamic Panel).

Add two *states* to the newly created *dynamic panel*, paste the elements and move the darker bubble to the second and third place to indicate the current page. Last but not least, label the *panel* and its *states*.

Note: I chose to build the page indicator with a *dynamic panel* with states for each highlight to show you how to assign *panel states* via *variables*. Alternatively, you can define a 'selected' *state* for each paging indicator, combine them in a *selection group* and use the swiping *event* to select one of them. You can see how this technique works in the 'Tabs' chapter.

Now, let's prototype the swiping behavior: since you reused the *dynamic panel* from the previous chapter, the 'OnSwipeLeft' and 'OnSwipeRight' *actions* are still there. But you need to add the *interactions* to update the header and the paging *panels*. You'll use the 'OnPanelStateChange' *event* of the content *panel* for this. Every time the content *panel state* changes the header and the paging indicator need to be updated.

First, store the current *panel state* of the content *panel* in a *variable*. You will use the *variable* value to update the header and the paging indicator *panels*. For this you'll use the 'OnPanelStateChange' *event*, which is called every time a *dynamic panel* changes its *state*.

Double-click on the 'OnPanelStateChange' *event* to add a new *case*. Select the 'Set Variable Value' *action* and add a new *variable* (e.g. 'currentPage') via the 'Add variable' link in the top-right corner. Set the checkbox for your newly created *variable* and use the ʹstate of panelʹ option from the dropdown to store the value of this *panel*. Now, every time the active *state* of your content *panel* is set, the name of the new *panel state* will be stored in your ʹcurrentPageʹ *variable*. You can now use this *variable* to update the other two *panel states*.

Add a 'Set Panel State' *action* to the 'OnPanelStateChange' *event* and select your header *panel* to be updated. Select 'Value' from the *state* dropdown and use the 'fx' button to open the 'Edit Value' dialog. Click the 'Insert Variable or Function...' link and choose the 'currentPage' *variable* and close the dialog. Create the same 'Set Panel State' *event* for the page indicator *panel*. The resulting *actions* should look like this:

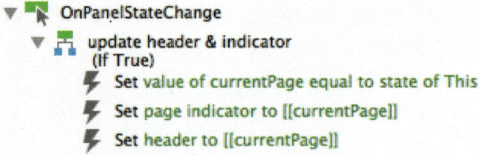

The content *panel* will now automatically trigger an update for the other two *panels*. The use of the 'currentPage' *variable* and the use of the 'OnPanelStateChange' *event* allows you to keep all *interactions* in one central place – the content *panel*. Changing the layout screen is now quite straightforward. New UI elements can be added to the screen and only the central *interaction* needs to be updated.

In the example file for this chapter I added a header button that will appear after you swiped to the second page, allowing you to jump back to the first screen. For this, I only had to add the button, make it initially invisible and add two *cases* to the 'OnPanelStateChange' *event* to hide and show them based on the active *panel state*.

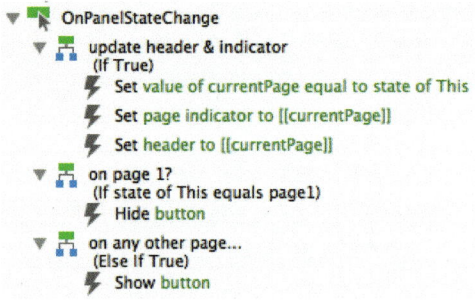

> **Note:** Using the 'OnPanelStateChange' event to control the behavior of your prototype is a very common pattern when building *panel*-based prototypes. Use it to initialize screens, trigger animations and transitions, etc. from there. You'll end up with various *cases* for the different screens (= *panel states*) on the main content panel.

```
▼ 📋 OnPanelStateChange
    ▶ 🔧 login
           (If state of This equals login)
    ▶ 🔧 activate
           (Else If state of This equals activate)
    ▶ 🔧 use case
           (Else If state of This equals use cases)
    ▶ 🔧 gui
           (Else If state of This equals gui)
```

Static Positioning

With Axure 6.5 a new function for *dynamic panels* was introduced: 'Pin to Browser'. It allows you to keep *panels* in a fixed position even though you are scrolling. Use this function to assign fixed positions for elements like headers, tabs or popup dialogs.

Select the content you want to 'pin', convert it into a *dynamic panel* and choose 'Pin to Browser' (right-click on a Dynamic Panel > Edit Dynamic Panel > Pin to Browser).

In the 'Pin to Browser' popup select the horizontal and vertical placement of the element. After you close the dialog a small pin will appear on the *panel.* Preview your prototype (press the F6 key on Windows or CMD+SHIFT+P on a Mac) to see it in effect.

  Note: If you only want to center-align content on a *page* (e.g. for a website prototype) use the 'Page Align' setting in the 'Page Style' tab instead of using the pin functionality.

9. Mobile UI Patterns

This chapter teaches you how to prototype the most common interaction paradigms of mobile apps and websites. These patterns will be the building blocks of your future prototypes.

As you will see, there is not one single right way to prototype something in Axure. The approach to choose depends on the problem at hand, on your personal preferences, etc. This chapter discusses different approaches on how to build the various patterns in Axure. It will explain the pros and cons for each option and teach you the most efficient way to build each pattern

If you are in a hurry you can just use the patterns from the provided source files, but I suggest that you take a look how the patterns are built. This will teach you 'Axure's way' of doing things and you'll learn how to create your own patterns. Plus, this is the most fun part of using Axure. Trust me…

Dialogs and Popups

A UI element you'll use in most of your prototypes is a dialog. This chapter will teach you how to build modal and non-modal dialogs and show you how to create overlays that slide into view.

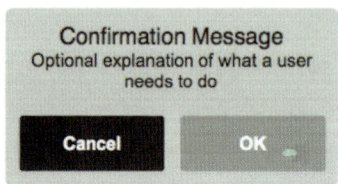

There are different ways to build a popup in Axure. You can layout your dialog, put it in a *dynamic panel* and tie *actions* to the buttons. But my suggestion is to turn all dialogs into *masters* thus allowing you to use *custom events*. This will simplify your *interactions* significantly since you'll have dedicated events for the dialog button options:

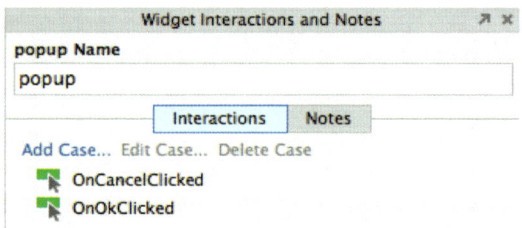

But you can decide later on if you want to build a *master*. Here is how to create a dialog in Axure: Start by layouting your dialog, select all its elements and convert it into a *dynamic panel* (right-click > Convert to Dynamic Panel). Don't forget to label the *panel* and its *state* (I usually give them the same name, e.g. 'popup'). Then, turn the *panel* invisible (click on the eye icon in the toolbar).

If you don't want to build a *master* you are done. Tie your interactions to the individual buttons of the dialog – but continue reading to see the benefits of using a *master*.

Using Masters and Custom Events

Now you want to use *custom events* to communicate which option the user selects. Select the *dynamic panel* and convert it into a *master* (right-click > Convert to Master). Double-click twice on it (first, to open the *master* and then to select its only *state*). Select the right button ('OK') and double-click on its 'OnClick' *event* to create a new *case*. Select the 'Raise Event' *action* from the bottom of the list and use the plus button to create two new *custom events* (I called mine 'OnCancelClicked' and 'OnOkClicked'):

Check the 'OnOkClicked' *event* checkbox and add a 'Show/Hide' *action* to hide your *dynamic panel*. The resulting *case* should look like this:

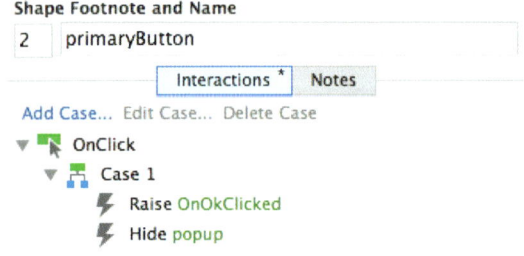

Copy the *case* over to the 'Cancel' button and change the *event* to be raised ('OnOkClicked'). Next, close both the *panel state* and the *master* view. Clicking on the *master* should reveal the newly created *events*.

To test your popup, add a button to the top-right corner of your screen that will show your popup when clicked.

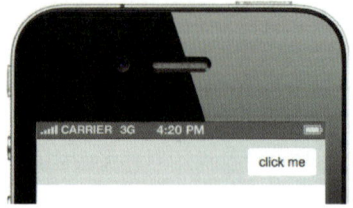

Use the button's 'OnClick' *event* and choose the 'Show' *action* for the popup. Select 'treat as lightbox' from 'More Options' and change the background color to 60% black (via the opacity slider). The resulting *case* should look like this:

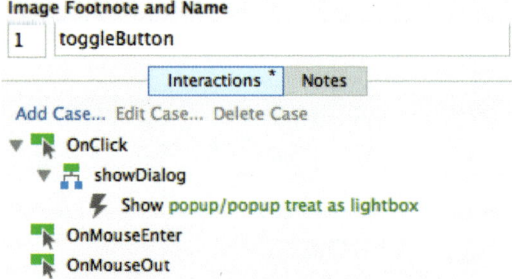

Combine Visibility and Placement

To make sure that your popup does not interfere with other elements, let's add a couple of *actions* to the *dynamic panel* containing the dialog.

First, you want to make sure that the *panel* is at the front when being shown. For this, double-click the 'OnShow' *event* and add a 'Bring to Front' *action*. You want to do the reverse for the 'OnHide' *event*: sending the *panel* to the back when hidden. The resulting *actions* should look like this:

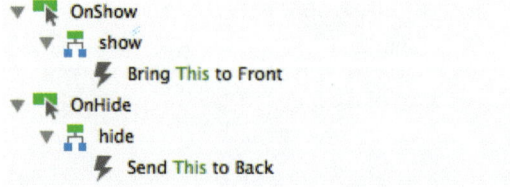

Note: I add these two *cases* to all *panels* I want to show and hide. They will then automatically take care of their placement.

Finally, to initialize your popup, add a 'Hide' *action* to the 'OnLoad' *event* of the *panel*. Now it will automatically be hidden and sent to the back.

 Note: If you briefly see the dialog when starting your prototype, the hide *action* of the 'OnLoad' *event* is too slow on your device. Just hide the *dynamic panel* in Axure before you run it and you are fine.

Make Them Modal

There is one more thing you might want to do to improve your overlay. But first, preview your prototype to check its behavior.

Clicking the dialog's buttons should hide it but so does clicking outside on the black 'fog of war'. That's because the 'lightbox' option of Axure creates a non-modal overlay (you can click anywhere outside the overlay to hide it). To make your dialog modal, simply add an invisible *rectangle* the size of your screen resolution to your dialog's *panel*. Put it below the dialog's elements and you won't be able to click on the 'fog of war' anymore.

Slide Content Into View

There are several UI elements in mobile user interfaces that slide in and out of view, e.g. on-screen keyboards and the notification *panels* of Android and iOS. This section will show you to prototype this behavior in Axure.

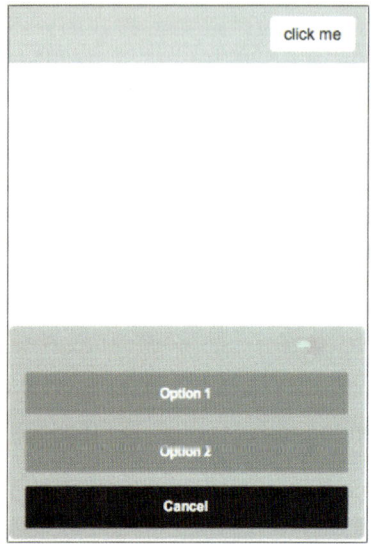

The way to build a sliding panel is similar to creating a dialog: Layout your panel, place it at the bottom of your screen, convert it into a *dynamic panel* and turn it into a *master*. Only its *interaction* is slightly different: Add a 'Show' *action* to the button's 'OnClick' *event* and use the 'slide up' animation from the animation dropdown. If you want, adjust the timing – the default is 500ms. The resulting *action* should look like this:

If you now preview your prototype (hide the *dynamic panel* first), the dialog should move into view.

Next you want to make its buttons interactive – you want to move the dialog out of view and raise a *custom event*. Double-click on the first button's 'OnClick' *event* and add a 'Hide' *action* with a 'slide down' animation (using the same timing as before).

Add a 'Wait' *action* with a similar delay to the *case* to tell Axure to wait until the animation has ended. Last but not least, raise a *custom event*. The resulting *case* should look like this:

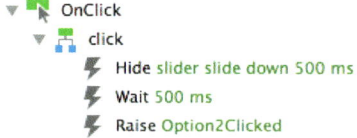

Add similar *actions* to the other buttons and you are almost done. As before, you need to add 'Bring to Front/Send to Back' *actions* to the 'OnShow' and 'OnHide' *events* and a 'Hide' *action* to the *dynamic panel's* 'OnLoad' *event* to initialize it.

 Note: If you want to make this dialog modal just increase the size of the *dynamic panel* to cover the full screen – as I did in the example file.

Combining Dialogs and Popups

To reduce the number of *dynamic panels* in your prototype you can combine all your dialogs in a single *panel*. To make this work you need to change each dialog's *interaction* a bit.

Put each dialog in a separate *panel state* and add an '.empty' *state* as the top-most one.

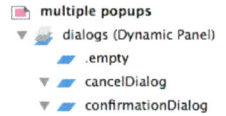

Use the *panel's* 'OnPanelStateChange' *event* to show and hide the *panel*. If the active *state* is '.empty' hide it and send it to the back, otherwise show it and bring it to the front.

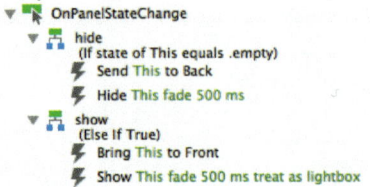

To close and hide a dialog (e.g. after clicking a button and triggering an *event*), set the *panel state* to '.empty'.

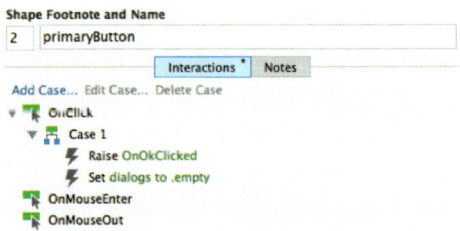

Now your *panel* is ready. To show a specific dialog just set the *panel* to the dialog's *state*.

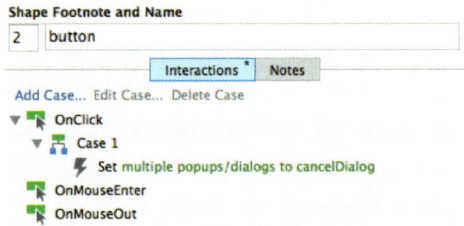

Use the *custom events* to determine what option the user clicked. If you use the same *custom event* in multiple dialogs you need to determine which dialog triggered it:

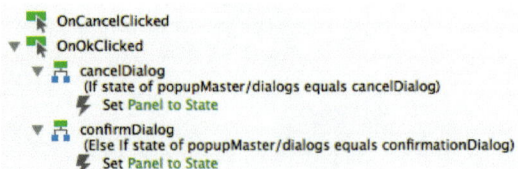

To simplify your prototype create unique *events* for each dialog:

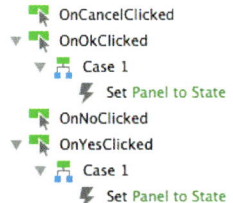

Now all your dialogs are kept inside a single *dynamic panel* reducing the number of *dynamic panels* in your prototype.

Text Fields and Forms

Before Axure 7.0 only text (and password) fields were part of Axure's widget library. Now you can differentiate the following input field types: text, password, email, number, phone number, URL and search fields. But not all available input types [081] are implemented (e.g. 'Date', 'Month' and 'Date and Time' are currently missing).

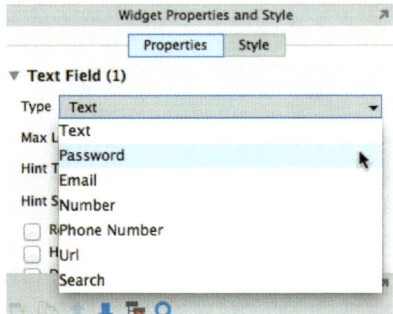

The advantage of using input field types is better usability because the onscreen keyboard reflects the text field input type, making it easier for your users to input the correct information. See the iOS keyboards below for a URL (the space bar is replaced by a slash and a domain button) and a phone number input field:

But input types do behave and look differently on different mobile operating systems. Mike Gray provided an overview in the Axure forums [240]:

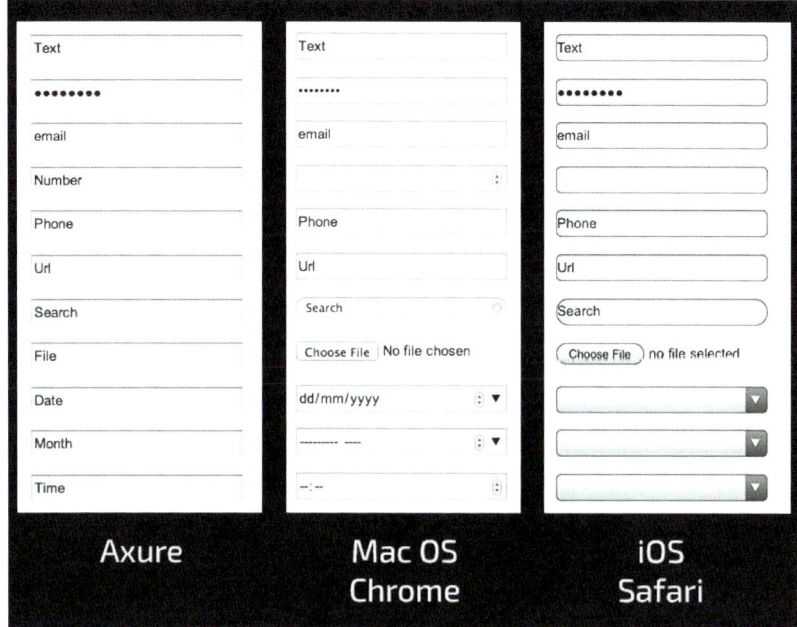

Focus on Load

Setting the focus on an input field is quite easy. Just use the 'OnLoad' *event* of the *page* or the 'OnPanelLoad' (or the 'OnPanelStateChange') *event* of the *panel* and use the 'Set Focus' *action*.

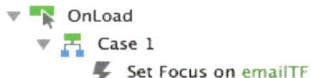

Specifying the Tab Order

To further improve the usability of your forms, specify the tab order of its elements. You define it through the stacking order ('bring to front', 'send to back', etc.) of your input fields: the bottom-most one is visited first. By looking at the 'Widget Manager' you can determine the (hidden) tab order of your elements. The top-most entry in the list is lowest in the stacking order (that's confusing, I know).

In the image below, the first element in the tab order is the 'emailTF', followed by the 'numberTF'.

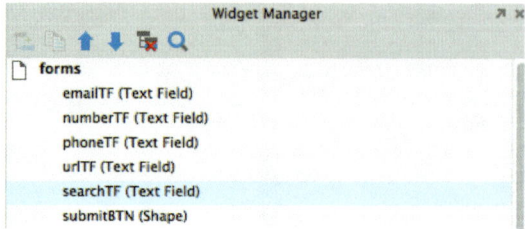

You can rearrange elements in the 'Widget Manager' via drag and drop or use the 'Bring Forward' (CMD+']' on a Mac and CTRL+']' on Windows) and the 'Send Backward' (CMD+'[' on a Mac and CTRL+'[' on Windows) commands.

To test the tab order in Axure, click on your canvas and use the tab key to tab through your elements.

Assigning a Submit Button

First, drag a button or a rectangle on your canvas and label it. Then, select all the elements of your form and use the 'Submit Button' dropdown in the 'Widget Properties' section to assign the submit button to your elements.

Forms and Gestures

In Axure 6.5. forms and gestures didn't play well together. If you added swiping or drag-and-drop *actions* to a *dynamic panel* containing form fields you weren't able to select the fields. The solution was to place your forms inside an extra *dynamic panel* – this meant adding an extra *sub-panel* for either the form fields or the gesture detection. But with Axure 7.0 this bug has been fixed.

Tabs

A tab bar is another common UI element used (not only) in mobile user interfaces. Let me show you how to build one in Axure.

Create the first tab by dragging a *rectangle* (e.g. 128x98px for five tabs on a retina iPhone) to the bottom-left corner of your *screen*. Next, define its active *state* via the 'Selected' *style* in the 'Widget Properties' section (e.g. change its background color). If you want, you can also define its 'pressed' state using the 'MouseDown' *style*.

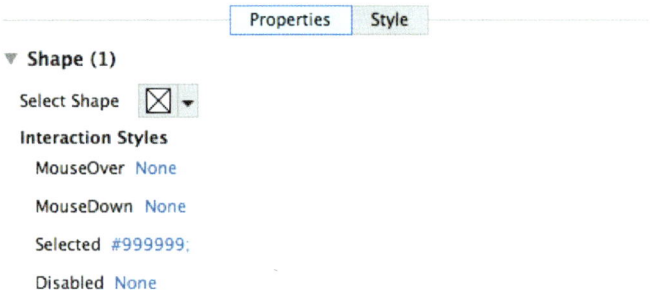

Next, you want to tell the tab to become selected when clicked. Double-click on the 'OnClick' *event* of the *rectangle* to create new *case*, assigning the 'Set Selected/Checked' *action* to itself.

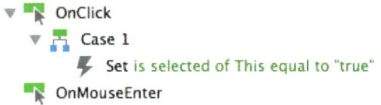

After you have defined its basic behavior, copy the tab and paste it four times next to each other to create a full tab bar.

one

Afterwards, define a *selection group* for the tabs so only one of them can be selected at a time. Select all five tabs, click in the 'Selection Group' dropdown in the 'Widget Properties' section and give your *selection group* a name. And don't forget to check the 'Selected' checkbox for the first tab to make it active. Last but not least, name each tab (e.g. 'tab1' to 'tab5').

In the next two sections you'll see how to best use a tab bar in *page* and *panel*-based prototypes.

Tabs for Page-based Prototypes

For a *page*-based prototype turn your tab bar into a *master* (right-click > Convert to Master), name it (e.g. 'page tabs') and hardcode the page to be opened by using the 'Open Page' *action* for each tab.

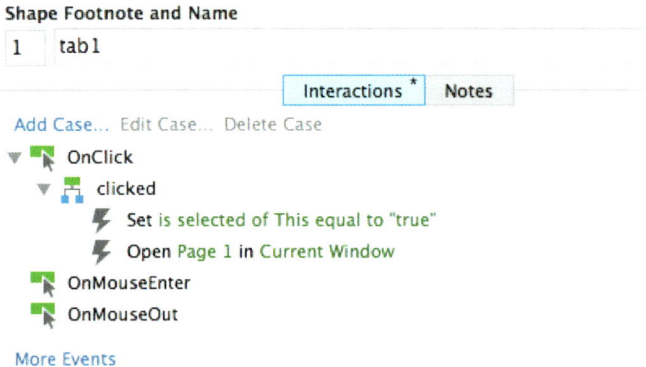

To ensure that the tab bar is always placed on the same location define the *master's* 'drop behavior' (right-click on the *master* > Lock to Master Location). Now the *master* will be placed at the x and y-coordinates you placed it inside the *master view*, e.g. at the bottom of your screen.

Last but not least, you need to set the highlight for the tab bar on each *page*. Use the *page's* 'OnPageLoad' event:

Copy this *case* to each *page* and adjust the tab to be selected. With this, your tab bar is done.

Tabs for Panel-based Prototypes

Place your your tab bar outside (and on top of) the *dynamic panel* that contains your prototype screens.

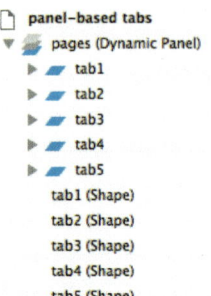

The easiest way to make your tab bar interactive is to add *interactions* to each tab. Use the 'OnClick' *event* to update the content *panel* accordingly.

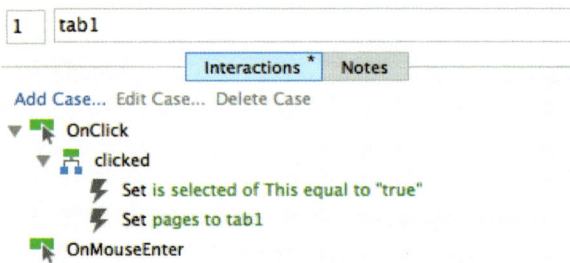

To further simplify your prototype I recommend to turn your tab bar into a *master* to be able to use *custom events*. You might think this is too much hassle – but bear with me, I think the result is worth the (one-time) extra effort.

Select all tabs and turn them into a *master* (right-click > Convert to Master). Open the *master* and double-click on the existing 'OnClick' *case* of the first tab to add two new *interactions* to it. Select the 'Raise Event' *action* and add a new *event* called 'OnTabClicked' and select it. This *event* will now be called when the user clicks on the tab.

Your *master* has now a way to communicate with the 'outside world.' But you also need to tell which tab was clicked. For this you'll use a *variable*. Add a 'Set Variable Value' *action* and define a new *variable* called 'activeTab' (use the 'Add Variable' link the top-right corner) and set it to '1' for the first tab.

The order of these two *actions* is important. First, you want to set the *variable* and raise the *event* afterwards. Change the order of the two *actions* if needed. The resulting *case* should look like this:

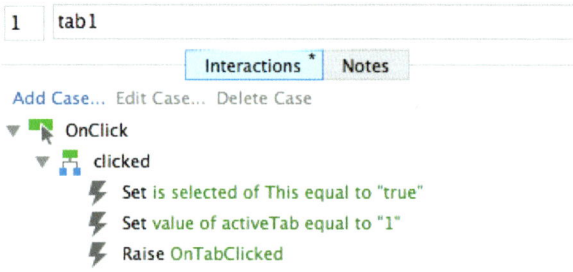

Now select the two new *actions* and copy and paste them to the 'OnClick' *events* of the other tabs. Change the 'set *variable* value' action to match its *value* to the tab number. When you are done, close the *master*. You'll see that the tab bar now offers a single (custom-made) event: 'OnTabClicked'.

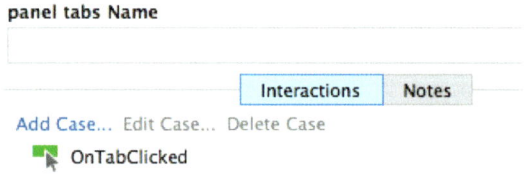

Here comes the cool part: Since Axure 6.5 you can use values (or expressions) to set the *panel state* of *dynamic panels*. This means that the n-th *panel state* will be set when you provide the value 'n'. This is quite powerful and simplifies your tab bar's *interactions* significantly. You can now use the 'activeTab' *variable* to set the *state* of your content *panel* with a single *action*:

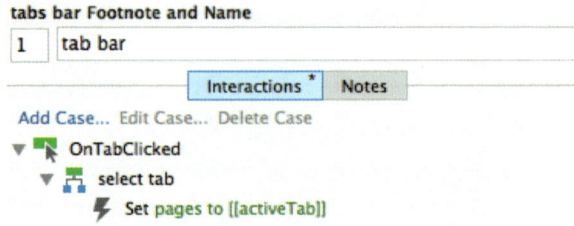

This works since the 'activeTab' *variable* contains the 'ID' of the clicked tab. (The order of your tabs and of your screens in the *panels* need to match, of course.)

To create this *case*, double-click on the 'OnTabClicked' *event* and choose the 'Set Panel State' *action* for the 'pages' *panel*.

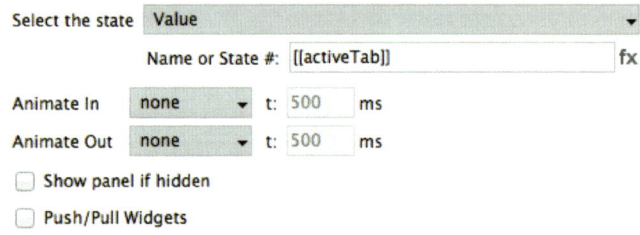

Choose 'Value' from the 'Select the state' dropdown and click on the 'fx' icon. In the 'Edit Value' tab click the 'Insert Variable or Function...' and select the 'activeTab' *variable* you defined previously.

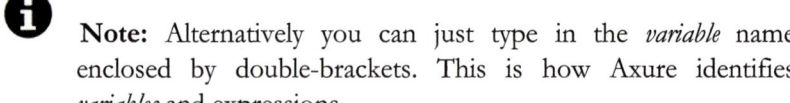 **Note:** Alternatively you can just type in the *variable* name enclosed by double-brackets. This is how Axure identifies *variables* and expressions.

Accordion Lists

Accordion lists are lists with clickable section headers – clicking expands or collapses the section below the header. Usually the first section is open by default while the other sections are closed. There are exclusive accordion lists, where only one header can be expanded at a time; and non-exclusive ones, where multiple headers can be opened simultaneously. Before Axure 7.0, prototyping this behavior was no fun at all. But a new feature called 'push/pull widgets' makes it really easy.

Let's start by laying out your first section of the list with its header expanded:

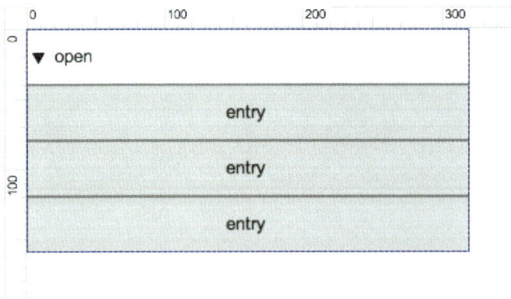

Turn the elements into a *dynamic panel* (select all entries and right-click > Convert to Dynamic Panel) and call this first *state* 'open'. Copy the header, create a second *state* called 'close', open it and paste the header inside. Change its layout a bit to indicate its closed *state* (e.g. use different triangles next to the title).

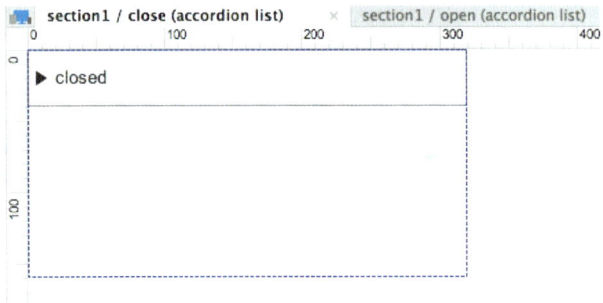

Close the *panel states* and make sure that the 'Fit to content' checkbox is set in the 'Panel Properties'. Now Axure will adjust the *panel's* size to its active *panel state's* content. Copy and paste this *panel* twice to create a list with three section. Rename the new *panels* and set their first *state* to 'close'. (Use the arrows in the 'Widget Manager' or drag the entry to the topmost position.) The resulting list should look like this:

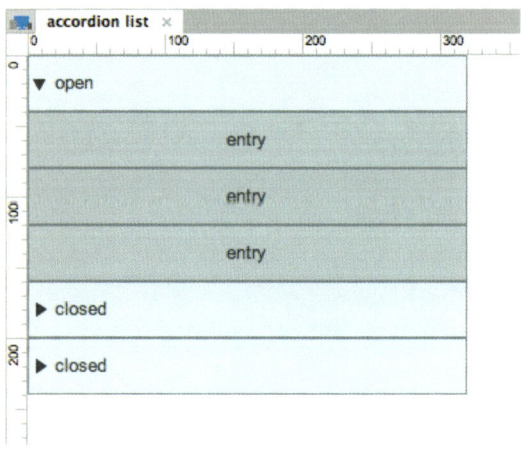

Make Them Interactive

You are going to use the new 'OnClick' *event* of each *dynamic panel*. Before Axure 7.0 only 'regular' *widgets* offered an 'OnClick' *event*.

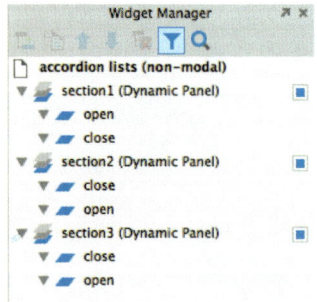

Double-click on the 'OnClick' *event* of the first *panel* and choose the 'Set Panel State' *action*. Select 'Next' from the dropdown and check the

'Wrap from last to first' checkbox. Since your *panel* has only two *state*s, it will now toggle between these two.

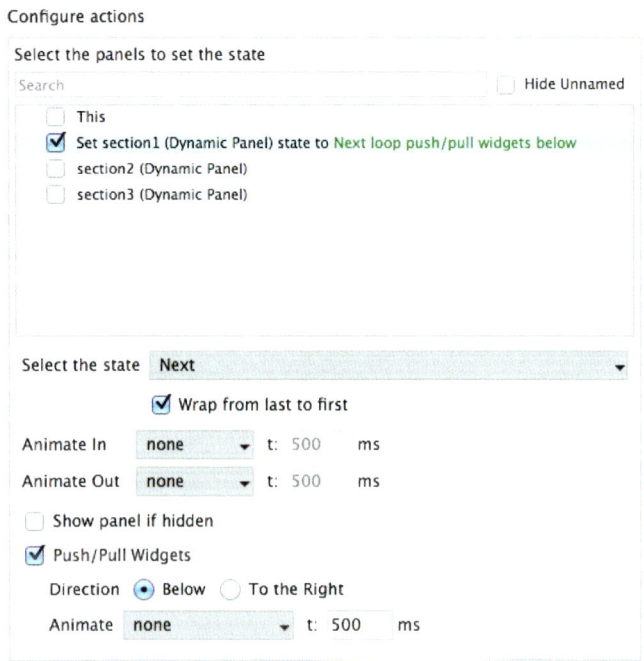

Last but not least, select 'Push/Pull Widgets' to tell Axure to push the other *panels* down. Your prototype will now automatically make room for the content of the opened section *panel*. The resulting *case* should look like this:

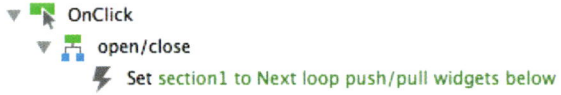

Repeat the procedure for each *panel* and you have created a non-exclusive accordion list.

Note: If you want to make the list elements interactive as well, use the 'OnClick' *event* of the (open and the closed) header instead using of the *panel* one. The *actions* remain the same.

Make Them Exclusive

If you want only one section open at a time, close all other sections (using the push/pull option) when you open the clicked one.

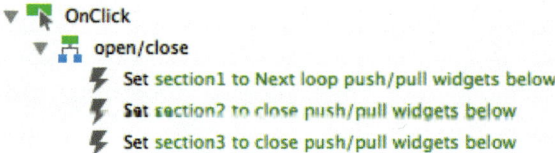

Add similar *actions* to the other *panels* and your accordion list has become 'exclusive'.

 Note: If a *panel* is already in the *state* you assign it to, the *action* (plus its animation) will not be executed. That's why you will only see the currently open header being closed in the example above. The other *panels* will ignore the close *action*.

Splash Screens

A lot of apps display a splash screen (showing the app's logo, the name of the app, a loading indicator, etc.) when they are opened.

On iOS you can use Axure's Mobile Settings to use a static image as a splash screen for your prototype. Since it's a static image you won't be able to animate your splash screen's content. That's why I recommend to add an extra *panel state* to your (*panel*-based) prototype to store your splash screen's content.

Make the splash screen the topmost *panel* of your prototype since it's the first screen to be shown. To automatically load a new screen after your splash screen was displayed use the 'OnLoad' *event* of your prototype's *dynamic panel*. To set the time for the splash screen to be displayed, use a 'Wait' and a 'Set Panel State' *action*.

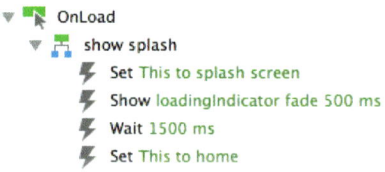

Alternatively, you could treat the splash screen as a full screen dialog (see 'Dialogs and Popups') that you show at the beginning.

 Note: If your prototype contains more than one use case you might want to add an entry page to your prototype to provide shortcuts to the different use cases.

Drag to Refresh

This pattern was first introduced by the 'Twitterific' twitter client and has now been widely adopted. The idea is that you drag down a list to refresh or update its content.

New capabilities of Axure 7.0 (the 'OnSwipeDown' *event* and pushing/pulling *widgets* when you toggle an element's visibility) have made it fairly easy to prototype this pattern.

Building the Refresh Indicator

Let's say you have a *panel* called 'content' containing your list entries. Place a small *rectangle* on top (e.g. 640x88px) and add an image showing a loading indicator (get one from `ajaxload.info` [153]).

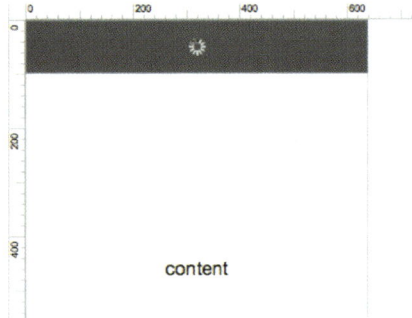

Name both of them (e.g. 'bg' and 'loadingIndicator'), select the loading indicator image and turn it invisible. Select both elements and turn them into a single *dynamic panel* (right-click > Convert to Dynamic Panel). Give it a decent name (e.g. 'updatePanel') and send it to the back.

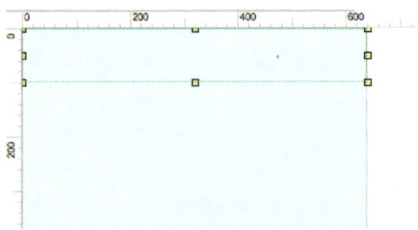

Making it Interactive

Next, let's add the *interactions* that moves your list down revealing the *panel*. Select the content *panel* and choose the 'OnSwipeDown' *event* hidden behind the 'More Events' link. Select the 'Show' *action* and tell the 'updatePanel' to slide down. In addition, tell the update *panel* to 'push down' the content *panel* using the same timing (e.g. 300ms).

When you now drag the panel down, your update *panel* will slowly be revealed.

Next, you want to show the loading indicator for a while and hide the 'updatePanel' afterwards. Select the *panel* and pick the 'OnShow' *event* from the 'More Events' list. Make the loading indicator visible, wait for a short time (e.g. two seconds) and hide it again. Afterwards hide the 'updatePanel' again, by reversing the previous defined animation ('slide up' and 'pull').

Before testing your prototype check the 'Prevent vertical page scrolling' checkbox in the 'Mobile/Device' settings. This prevents your *page* from scrolling down when the user swipes. With this, the 'drag to refresh' should work.

Triggering Events

The only thing that is still missing, is how to trigger new *actions* based on this *event*. The easiest way is to add additional *actions* to the 'OnSwipeDown' *event* of the *panel*, following the 'Wait' *action*.

But if you plan to reuse this element, I recommend turning it into a *master* (right-click > Convert to Master) and adding a *custom event* (e.g. 'OnDragDown'). This will simplify your *interactions*, since you introduce a dedicated *event* to work with.

For more details on how to build *custom events*, take a look at the 'Tab Bar' chapter.

Lists with Selection Highlight

iOS uses a nice animation effect when navigating between lists: selecting a list entry highlights it, and the current screen slides out to the left while the new one slides in. You can see this behavior for example in the iOS 'Music' app. I'll show you how to prototype this behavior in Axure using *dynamic panel state* animations and button *states*.

First, drag several plain buttons onto your screen and align them vertically. Select the top one and click on the grey circle to give it rounded corners on the top. Do the same for the bottom button (for its bottom corners).

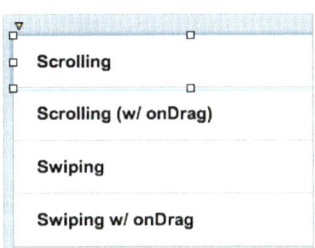

Next, create the highlight *state* (white font and blue background) by defining the look and feel for the first button's 'selected' *state* (right-click > Edit Button Shape > Edit Selected Style).

Once you have defined a style, a 'dog ear' will appear in the top left corner of the button. Now you can copy the style to the other buttons by using Axure's 'Format Painter' (the paint brush with the blue ink).

Next, define the button's highlight behavior. If a button is pressed you want to set it to 'selected' to show the highlight. Change the *panel state* of your prototype (slide both *states* in and out to the left), wait for the transition to end and reset the button *state* afterwards:

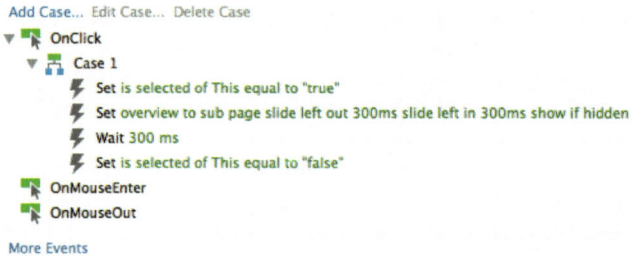

On the new page, place a 'Back' button that uses the sliding animation (in the opposite direction) to return the user to the list.

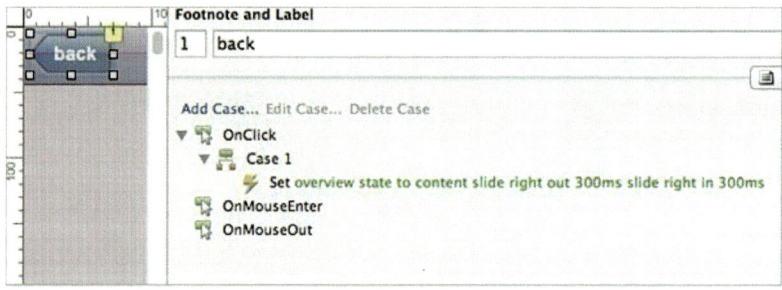

Note: Usually the 'selected' *style* is used to highlight a single element of a group, e.g. the selected tab of a tab bar. To group the elements select them and define a *selection group* (right-click > Edit Button Shape > Assign Selection Group). You can skip this step here since you always leave the screen after the selection.

Now your list elements will show which entry has been clicked.

Sliding Menus

Quite a few apps feature a menu button in the top-left corner to slide its content to the right, revealing a menu. Take for example the following iOS apps: 'Facebook', 'Path', 'Nike Running' or 'Sparrow'. In the first edition of this book this was the most complex pattern to build. With the 'push/pull' capabilities of Axure 7.0 prototyping this pattern has become quite easy to prototype.

Building the Menu

Let's start with laying out the menu: put a header on top of your *page* (e.g. 640x88px for a iOS retina phone) and place a button in the left corner. Place a *dynamic panel* below the header and add *panel states* for each screen you want to access via the menu.

Don't forget to put some placeholder content on each *panel* to differentiate them and label the *panel* and its *states*. In this example I'll use three screens:

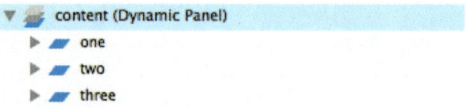

Place another *dynamic panel* on top – this *panel* will contain the menu. Reduce its width by 80px (to 560px for an iOS retina phone) to be able to see the toggle button when the menu is visible. Open it's *panel state*, give it a dark background, add a header and add three menu entries.

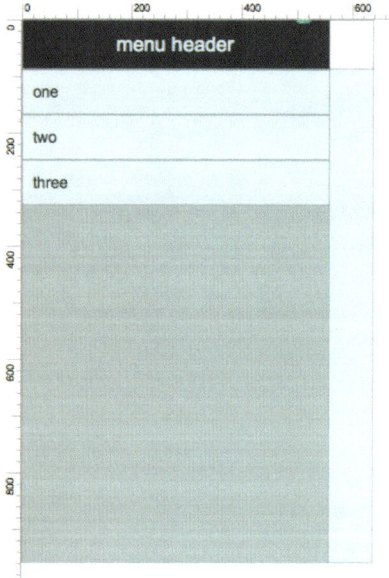

Select the three entries, define a 'Selected' *style* in the 'Widget Properties and Style' for them, left-align their text and add some padding to the left.

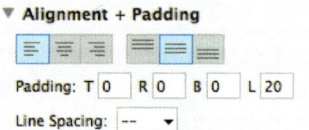

Assign them to a *selection group* (to make sure that only one of them can be selected at a time), label each of them and set the 'Selected' checkbox for the first entry to match the highlight to the active *state* of your content *panel*.

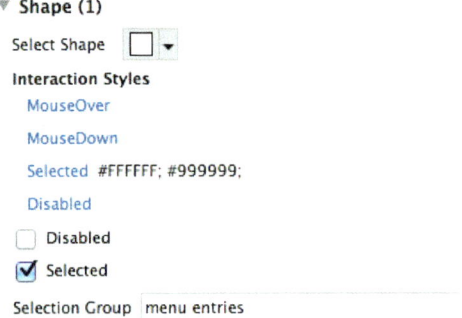

Next, turn the menu *panel* invisible and send it to the back of your prototype. And don't forget to label all your elements (header, button, content and menu entries) because you'll need to access them in your *interactions*.

Make it Interactive

Let's start with the menu button: create a 'Selected' *style* for the button to communicate its pressed state.

Add an 'OnClick' *event* to the button to toggle this *state*.

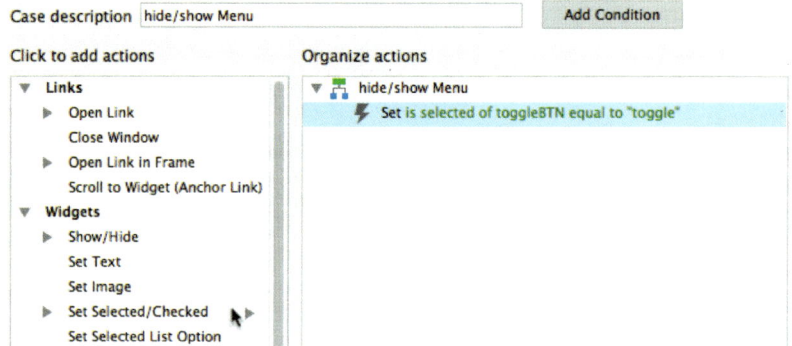

 Note: Do not use the 'This Widget' identifier for the *action*, use its real name instead (in my case 'toggleBTN') because you'll recycle the *case* and copy it to other elements.

Next, add a second *action* to toggle the visibility of the menu and tell the *widget* to push/pull the other elements to the right.

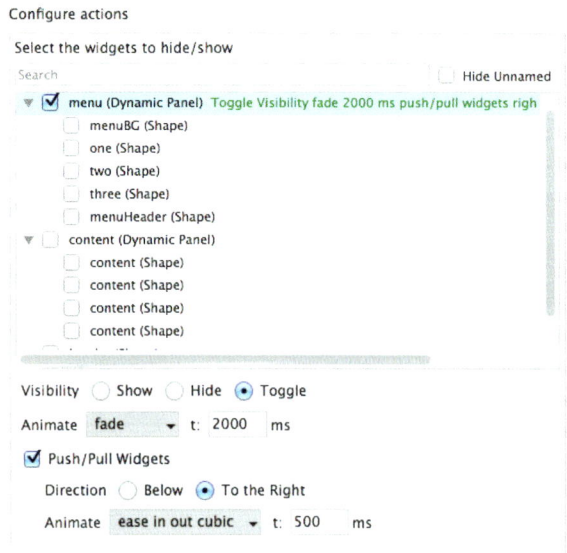

Configure actions

Select the widgets to hide/show

To create the sliding effect for the menu you need to animate this *action* (use a 500ms 'ease in and out'). But you don't want to have the menu disappear instantly, thus you want to apply a longer delay for the visibility toggle (e.g. two seconds). The resulting *case* should look like this:

The button is now functional, allowing you to show and hide the menu. Next, you want to enable swiping gestures on the content *panel* to hide and show the menu. Copy the *case* you defined for the button and add it to the 'OnSwipeLeft' and 'OnSwipeRight' *events* of the content *panel*. And don't forget to change the name of the *actions*.

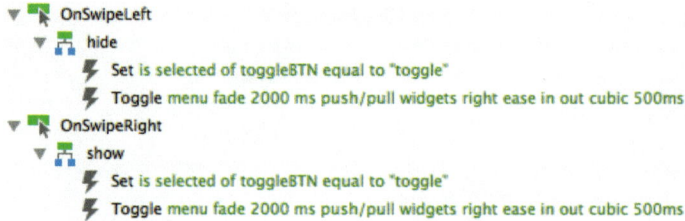

Next, let's make the menu entries clickable: double-click on the *panel state* of the menu *panel* in the 'Widget Manager' to open it. Select the first menu entry and double-click on its 'OnClick' *event* to create a new *case*. First, activate its selected *state* and update the *panel state* of the content *panel* to show the selected page.

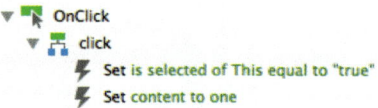

Copy this *case* and paste it to all other menu entries and update the 'SetPanelState' *action*.

When you now test your prototype, you'll see that clicking a menu entry will change the page but the content *panel* does not slide back (yet). To achieve this, simply add two *actions* you defined before to the 'OnPanelStateChange' *event* of the content *panel* (copy & paste is your friend).

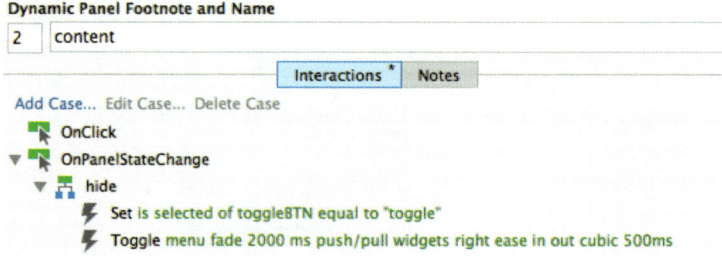

Updating the content *panel* will now tell the *panel* to slide back. But clicking the selected menu entry does not close the menu.

The reason for this is that clicking a selected entry tells the content *panel* to change to an already set *state*. Thus the 'OnPanelStateChange' *event* will not be triggered and the menu remains open. To fix this you need to introduce a new *panel state* to the content *panel*. Add an empty *panel state* to the bottom and label it (e.g. 'empty').

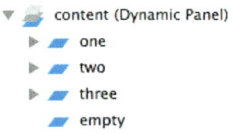

Use this *state* as a stepping stone to trigger the 'OnPanelStateChange' *event*. Always set the *panel* to the empty *state* before changing to the correct *state*. This way the 'OnPanelStateChange' *event* will always be triggered.

Last but not least, you want the menu to remain open when the empty *state* content gets activated. For this you need to add a *condition* to the menu *panel's* 'OnPanelStateChange' *event* excluding it.

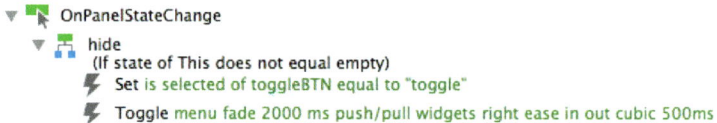

Select the content *panel*, double-click on the 'OnPanelStateChange' *case* you defined and press the 'Add Condition' button. There, set it to only call the *action* when its current *state* is not the 'empty' one. And that's it.

Note: If you plan to have different headers for your sub *pages*, put them all into a *dynamic panel* (instead of the single header element) and update its *panel state* via the 'OnClick' *events* of your menu entries. See the 'Swiping' chapter for an example.

Fullscreen on Scroll

Recently a new UI pattern emerged for apps that offer a long list of content: the scrollable fullscreen mode. When the user scrolls down, the app hides its header, footer and toolbars to show its content in full view. When the user stops and scrolls up, the toolbars re-appear. This trick allows you to present content in a fullscreen view and to also offer a list of global functions. With Axure 7.0 you can prototype this pattern using the newly introduced scrolling *events* and *variables*. Two new *events* allow you to determine if the user scrolls: 'OnScroll' for *panels* and 'OnWindowScroll' for *pages*. The *events* are called for each pixel the user scrolled – that means if the user scrolled down 500 pixels the *event* will be called 500 times.

Unfortunately, the scrolling direction is not communicated via these events. You have to determine this yourself. Use the 'Window.ScrollY' *variable* containing the current y-position of your content (or its counterpart for the x value, of course) to determine the scroll direction. Store its value in a *variable* and compare it to its current value when the *event* is called again. If the old value is greater than the current one, the user scrolls up. If it is smaller, they scroll down. Use the same approach to detect horizontal scrolling

Let's create a hideable header on a *page* to demonstrate the concept. First, create a scrollable *page*: Put a *placeholder widget* on the *page*, position it at (0, 0), make it as wide as your screen and really long, e.g. 5000 pixels. Place your header on top, turn it into a *dynamic panel* (right-click > Convert to Dynamic Panel) and give it a reasonable name (e.g. 'header').

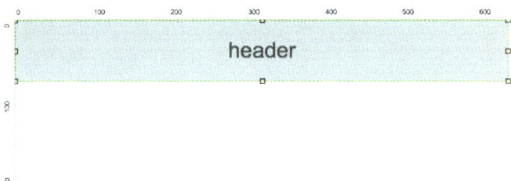

To keep it on top use the 'Pin to browser' function in the 'Widget Properties', select 'top left' and uncheck the 'Keep in Front' checkbox.

Next, let's hide and show the header. You need to slide the header up when the user scrolls down (and vice versa). Double-click on the 'OnWindowScroll' *event* of the current *page*, click the 'Add condition' button and select the 'Value of a variable' option from the dropdown. Next, select 'Add new' and create a new *variable* called 'lastY'.

The header needs to be hidden when the *variable's* value is less than the *variable* value of 'Window.ScrollY'. Click on the 'fx' icon and select 'Window.ScrollY' in the variable dropdown (or type its name with double square brackets in the text field). Close the 'Condition Builder', select the 'Hide' *action* for your header *panel* and select to slide the header upwards (e.g. in 300ms):

Copy and paste this *case* and reverse its *condition* and *action* for the upward scroll.

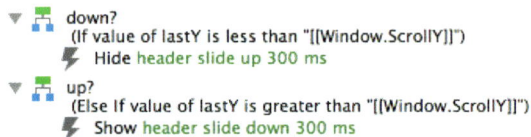

Add a third *case* to store the current 'Window.ScrollY' value in your 'lastY' *variable*. Reverse it to an IF (right-click on the *case* > Toggle IF/ ELSE IF), to make sure it is always executed and store the current y-position in your 'scrollY' *variable*:

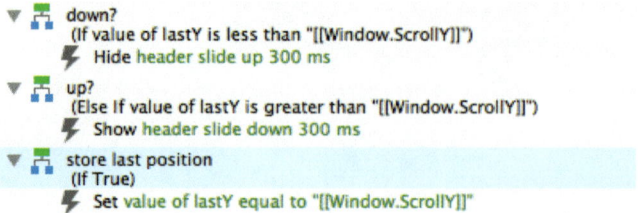

Now your header should scroll in and out of view depending on your scrolling direction.

If you test the prototype you will notice (maybe not – it depends on your mobile OS) that the header will disappear if you scroll beyond the top of your *page* when the content snaps back to the top. This can be fixed by adding a second *condition* to the downward scroll *case*. Check if the 'Window.ScrollY' *variable* is greater than '0' (negative values mean that you have 'scrolled over the top').

Note: To simplify this example you can use the 'scrollDetector' which I explain in detail in the 'Detect Scrolling' chapter. It offers *events* for the different scrolling possibilities. Here is how to use its *events* for our example:

Sticky Headers for Lists

Lists on iOS (there they are called 'TableViews' [158]) use a nice interaction paradigm. When you use headers within a list, the active category header stays on top of your *page* while you scroll. This means you always know what category is currently the topmost one – even if you cannot see its header.

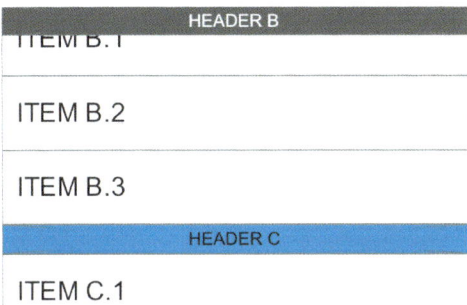

Prototyping this functionality was a bit cumbersome but with Axure 7.0 it has become quite straightforward. Let's use the 'scrollDetector' which I explain in full detail in the 'Detect Scrolling' chapter.

First, build your list using Axure's *rectangle widget*. Create a couple of headers with list items below.

Building the Header

Next, turn the top-most header into a static *dynamic panel* that 'recognizes' the currently active section. Copy the header, then right-click and turn it into a *dynamic panel*. Give the *panel* as many *states* as you have sections in your list and paste the header into each *state*. Update the header to match it to your section titles. And don't forget to label the *panel* and its *states* accordingly.

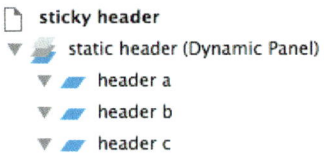

To make sure that the top-most header stays on top, click the 'Pin to Browser' link in the 'Widget Properties' and select 'top left'.

Storing the Section Coordinates

Next, you want to store the y-position of the section headers in *variables* since you will use the 'OnScroll' *event* and the 'Window.ScrollY' *variable* of Axure to determine what section is currently on top.

You can skip the first header because you already know its y-position – it's '0'.) Double-click on the 'OnPageLoad' *event* of the active *page* and choose a 'Set Variable Value' *action*. Click the 'Add variable' link in the top-right corner and create one for your second header (e.g. 'hbY'). Click the 'fx' button to assign the y-position of the header to it. Create a *local variable* (Axure suggests to use 'LVAR1') via the link in the bottom half and assign the header *widget* to it.

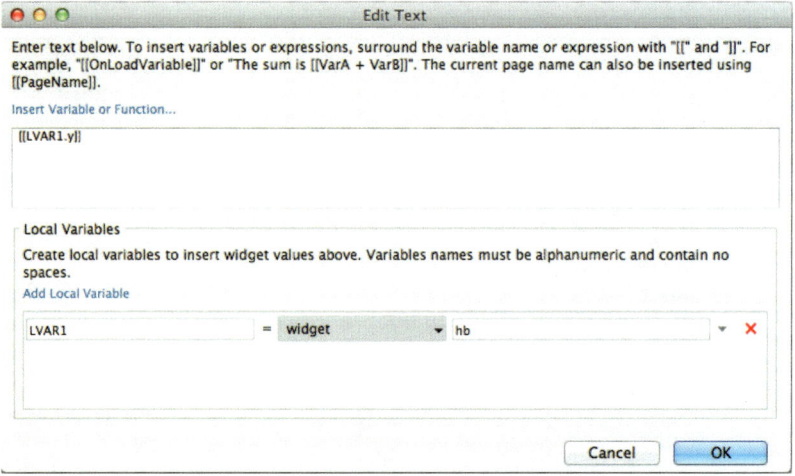

Click the 'Insert Variable or Function' link and select your new *variable*. Its name will be inserted in brackets in the text field. Add a '.y' after the *variable* name (inside the brackets) to get the y-coordinate of the header. Close the dialog. Repeat this for all other headers – your resulting *actions* should look like this:

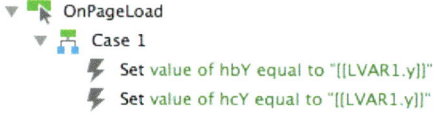

Using the Scroll Detector

Now you want to use the 'scrollDetector' which I introduce in the 'Detect Scrolling' chapter to track the user's scrolling behavior.

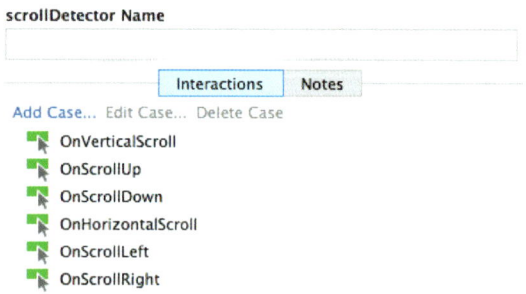

Use the 'OnVerticalScroll' *event* to determine which section of your list is currently on top of your screen. You only need to compare the y-coordinate of your window, stored in the '[[Window.ScrollY]]' *variable*, with the y coordinates of your headers. Depending on its value update the *panel state* of the static header on top.

Drag the 'scrollDetector' *master* on your canvas and start with the bottommost header, which has the largest y-value. Double-click on the 'OnVerticalScroll' *event* and press the 'Add Condition' button. Check whether the value of the '[[Window.ScrollY]]' *variable* is greater than the value '[[hcY]]'.

If this *condition* is met, set the 'header c' as the active *panel state* of your 'static header' *panel*. The resulting *interaction* should look like this:

Copy and paste the *interaction* and check for the y-coordinate of the next header and update the 'Set panel state' *action* accordingly. Work your way up to the first one. The resulting *interactions* should look like this:

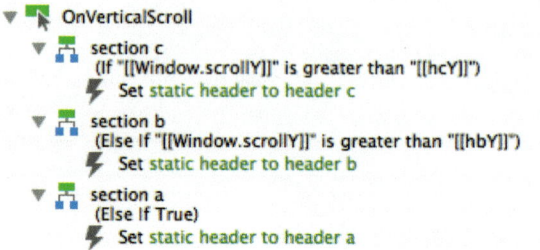

Now your static header will display which the section of your list is currently on top.

10. Advanced Topics

This chapter discusses several techniques to further enhance your Axure prototypes.

Using Webfonts

Each mobile platform has its unique platform-specific font(s): iOS uses 'Helvetica Neue' (and provides quite a few additional fonts), Android uses 'Droid Sans' and 'Roboto', Windows Phone uses 'Segoe' and Firefox OS uses 'Fira'.[1] If you want to use any other fonts in your prototype you can use the webfont functionality of Axure 7.0. Webfonts are online fonts you can embed into Axure's HTML output. There is a wide selection of free and commercial webfonts available[2].

Using Existing Webfonts

You can define webfont to be included in your prototype in the 'Web Fonts' section (Publish > Generate HTML). Name the font and either enter the link to the CSS webfont definition or paste the CSS statement there. Usually the webfont service will provide you a link to the font's CSS file.

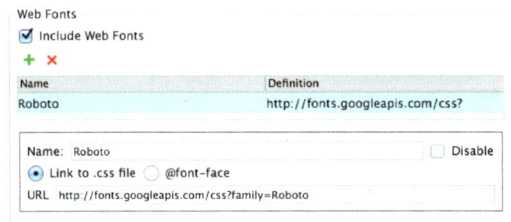

Alternatively, you can use the CSS definition provided by the webfont provider and paste it in the font-face text box.

Once you have added a webfont definition, type its name in the font dropdown to use it.

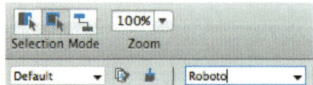

 Note: To state the obvious: your prototype needs to be online to access your webfonts.

If the fonts are available for download, install them on your computer. Then you'll be able to see them in Axure (e.g. 'Droid Sans' [147] and 'Roboto' [148] for Android or 'Segoe' (.zip – 88mb) [149] for Windows Phone) when you build your prototype.

If you want to include a font in your prototype that is not available as a webfont (but you have it on your computer), you can manually 'turn' it into a webfont. You can add the font to your prototype, upload it to an online location (e.g. to your Dropbox) or you can embed it into your Axure source file. (But please make sure that you have the property rights to use the font online.)

Using Local Fonts

You can use fonts in your prototype that you manually add to your prototype's HTML folder. Place the font files inside your prototype's HTML output directory, select the '@font-face' option, name your font and enter the following text in the text box:

```
font-family: yourFontName;
src: url(file:./yourFontFile) format("truetype");
```

 Note: The above example assumes that you use a TrueType font. If not, replace the format type with the correct format for your font: 'woff', 'embedded-opentype' or 'svg'.

Hosting Custom Fonts Online

Upload your font to an (accessible) online location, copy its URL and open the 'Web Fonts' section (Publish > Generate HTML). Select the '@font-face' option, name your font and enter the following text in the text box:

```
font-family: yourFontName;
src: url(theURLtoYourFont) format("truetype");
```

Embedding Custom Fonts

With this approach you'll insert the font (and not only its definition) to your prototype via CSS. This will increase the size of your prototype by the font file size – and yes, this is a hack.

First, you have to convert your font into a CSS-friendly format. For this use the online base64encoder [150] from Geoff Taylor. Upload the font and convert it – the result should be a very, very long block of text. Open the 'Web Fonts' dialog, select the '@font-face' option and enter the following text in the text box:

```
font-family: yourFontName;
src: url(data:font/ttf;base64,yourEncodedFontText)
   format("truetype");
```

Make sure to replace the name of the webfont and add the base64 encoded text.

 Note: The above example assumes that you use a TrueType font. For other font data formats take a look at the article 'Font-Face and Base64 Data-URL' [151].

You'll notice that the 'Generate HTML' dialog will become significantly slower – that's because it's not designed to handle large amounts of text, like the font definition you just pasted in there.

Tweaking Axure's HTML

I'll start with the bad news: there is no option for editing the HTML, CSS and JavaScript code of your prototypes within Axure. The good news is that there are ways to add web content to your prototype.

Using Inline Frames

The easiest way to add content to your prototype is using an *inline frame* (see the 'Embedding External Content' chapter).

Using AxShare

If you use AxShare to host your prototype you can add content to the header, body and to *dynamic panels*. Visit '`share.axure.com`', choose a hosted prototype of yours and paste your code in the 'plugins' sections. For more information take a look at this forum post [244] by Paul Sharer.

Adding Content to Your HEAD

You can use the 'Mobile/Device Settings' to inject code to the prototype headers as Axure. Yes, this is code injection – but for a good cause. Use the 'User Scalable' field in the 'Mobile Settings' and paste this into it:

```
no"/>YourContent<meta param="
```

Using JavaScript in Actions

You can use the 'Open Link' *action* of widgets to execute JavaScript. Paste the code you want to add in the hyperlink field:

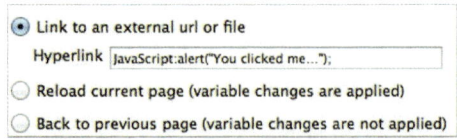

I used this hack and some jQuery to build the CSS dropin. For more details take a look at this [248] and this [249] forum post.

Embedding External Content

Inline frames allow you to embed HTML pages (local or web) into your prototype.[3] You can include all kinds of content via this method, e.g. ready-made content from other web services (like YouTube) or use services like the 'Google Chart API' [159] to generate results for you.[4] In the following example you'll include a Google Maps page in your prototype.

First, create an *inline frame* with the dimension of your prototype's screen size and place it at (0, 0). Remove the border (right-click > Edit Inline Frame > Toggle Border) to make the *frame* invisible and, depending on the content, you might also want to disable the scrollbars (right-click > Edit Inline Frame > Never Show Scrollbars).

Next, open Google Maps in your browser and type in any place you like (e.g. Langeoog). Zoom until you like the displayed section of the map, then click the link symbol and copy the HTML code in the second text box labeled 'Paste HTML to embed in website'.

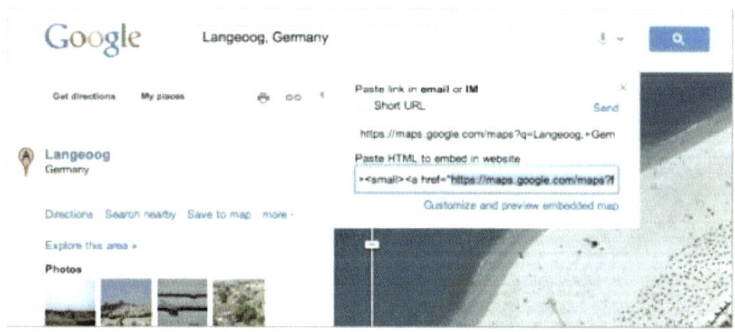

Copy the URL given in the 'href' attribute, double-click the *inline frame*, select the 'Link to external url or file' and paste the URL. Now the *inline frame* will display the Google Maps selection.

 Note: To hide the search result indicator of Google Maps you have to remove the following part from the link: 'q=langeoog, +germany&'.

Embedding Videos

The easiest way to embed a video in your prototype is to create a HTML page containing the video player code and add it via an *inline frame* to your prototype.

First, create an *inline frame* matching the video's dimension and place it at (0, 0). Remove the border (right-click > Edit Inline Frame > Toggle Border) to make the *frame* invisible and hide the scroll bars (right-click > Edit Inline Frame > Never Show Scrollbars). If you double-click on the *inline frame* you can enter a link to an external file. Let's use '_video_playback.html'. When you don't enter a URL or a file path (as you just did) the file needs to be inside the prototype's output directory.

Now you need to create the HTML for video playback. Open the text editor of your choice, copy the following code into it and save the file as '_video_playback.html' in your prototype's output directory.

```
<!doctype html>
<html>
<head>
 <title>HTML5 Video</title>
 <meta charset="utf-8" />
</head>
<body style="margin:0; padding:0; height:100%;
width:100%;" >
 <video id="video" width="320" height="480"
controls="controls">
 <source src="movie.mp4" />
 </video>
 <script type="text/javascript">
    var video = document.getElementById('
    video.addEventListener('click', function(){
        video.play();
    },false);
 </script>
</body>
</html>
```

The code above contains the HTML5 'video' and 'source' tags that make up the video player. It contains some additional JavaScript code, which I'll explain later.

Enter the path or the URL of your video file in the 'source' tag. If you want to use a local file, place it inside your prototype's output directory. Adjust the width and height values in the 'video' tag to match them to the video's dimensions. You can also add additional attributes to customize the video playback (show player controls, loop the video, etc.). For details on the HTML video attributes (preload, controls, autoplay, loop, muted, poster, src, height, width) visit the W3C School page [241].

Unfortunately all mobile platforms offer different levels of attribute conformity:[5]

- Starting with version 4.2, **iOS** does not allow you to 'preload', 'autoplay' or 'loop' your video. Thus the user needs to click the video's controls to start its playback, so always enable controls ('controls="controls")' on iOS.
- Prior to **iOS 4.0** two video tag bugs existed: if your 'video' tag contained a 'poster' attribute or if the first source statement was not the .mp4 one the video would not be displayed (that's why I omitted the 'type' attribute in the example above).
- Prior to **Android 2.3** the 'type' attribute in the 'source' tag broke the video. Both the 'autoplay' and the 'controls' attributes did not work (that's why I added some JavaScript to play the video when the user clicks on it). Current Android versions supports the .mp4 files.[6]
- **Windows Phone** does not support the 'preload' and the 'autoplay' attributes.[7] A video will always be shown as full screen and showing controls. The 'width' and 'height' attributes only affect the size of the 'poster' image.

ℹ️ **Note:** Since videos are displayed in full screen mode on mobiles you cannot overlay it with other content.

Note: If you want to automatically playback a video file (by using the 'autoplay' attribute) you need to set the HTML source to the *inline frame* when you want to start the video. For this use the 'Open Link(s) in Frame(s)' *action*.

Otherwise the video will be played as soon as the *panel* containing the *inline frame* is loaded – that is, when you open your prototype. Use the same method (open an empty HTML page) when you want to end your video playback early.

Supported Video File Formats

Let's briefly talk about video file format details. iOS [162], Android [161], Windows Phone [160] and Firefox OS [242] all support the same video format (H.264/MPEG 4).

To convert your video to .mp4 you can use free software like 'Miro Video Converter', 'VLC', 'Handbrake' or my preferred tool, the Firefox 'Firefogg' plugin. When encoding your file set the video format to 'H. 264'. The data rate setting (impacting the quality and file size) is up to you – I'd keep it below 1024 kb/s (Android recommends 500kb/s). For the audio format choose MPEG 4, set the data rate to 128 kb/s and the sample rate to 44,100 kHz.

Note: If you want to show your prototype on Firefox (below version 3.6) you need to create an .ogg (Ogg-Theora)[8] video file. For Opera you need to use a .webm file. Just add additional 'source' tag statements for the additional formats **below line 9 in** the HTML file:

```
<source src="movie.ogg" type="video/ogg" />
<source src="movie.webm" type="video/webm" />
```

Both formats can be created with the 'Firefogg' converter. For Internet Explorer you need Flash – but explaining this is beyond the scope of this book.[9]

Embedding Audio Files

The method to add audio files is similar to adding videos: use an *inline frame* and create an HTML page that uses the HTML5 'audio' tag. But it is easier to include audio files since there are fewer browser differences to consider.

As described in the previous chapter, create an *inline frame* and link to an HTML file with the following content:

```
<!doctype html>
<html>
<head>
 <title>HTML5 Audio</title>
 <meta charset="utf-8" />
</head>
<body style="margin:0; padding:0; height:100%;
width:100%;" >
 <audio id="audio" preload="none"
controls="true">
 <source src="audio.mp3" type="video/mp3" />
 <source src="audio.ogv" type="video/ogg" />
 </audio>
 <script type="text/javascript">
     var audio = document.getElementById('audio');
 video.addEventListener('click',function(){
         audio.play();
     },false);
 </script>
</body>
</html>
```

The audio tag supports additional attributes to customize the playback (show player controls, loop the video, etc.). For details on the HTML audio attributes (`preload`, `controls`, `autoplay`, `loop`, `src`) visit the W3C School page [164] .

As with the video tag, **Windows Phone** and **iOS** will not allow you to use the '`autoplay`' attribute. Thus include the '`controls`' attribute to allow the user to start the playback manually.

Supported Audio File Formats

All modern mobile browsers can playback either .mp3 or .ogg files, so create both to be safe. The later can be created with the 'Firefogg' converter.

Using HTML5 Caching

HTML5 allows you to cache web pages in your browser.[10] This means that the website will be stored by your browser when you view it, thus an internet connection is not required when you re-open the page. And with a few steps Axure prototypes can be made cacheable.

First, you need to create a so-called 'manifest file' listing all the files to be cached. Use the online tool 'manifestr' [171] (it provides an online bookmarklet) to create a cache manifest file for your prototype. Run your prototype and click the bookmarklet link. It will open an overlay containing the manifest file's content.

 Note: You need to create a manifest file for every page you want to cache. This is why *panel*-based prototypes are well suited for caching as they consist of a single page.

Copy its content and remove the leading file path from all files via 'Search and Replace' leaving only a slash ('/'), i.e. the output directory of your prototype.

```
 9
10    #internal HTML documents
11
12
13    #style sheets
14    file:///Users/lennart/Documents/Axure/Prototypes/Axure%20for%20Mobile/plugins/page_notes/styles/
15    file:///Users/lennart/Documents/Axure/Prototypes/Axure%20for%20Mobile/plugins/sitemap/styles/sit
16    file:///Users/lennart/Documents/Axure/Prototypes/Axure%20for%20Mobile/resources/css/default.css
17    file:///Users/lennart/Documents/Axure/Prototypes/Axure%20for%20Mobile/resources/css/reset.css
18
19    #style sheet images
20    file:///Users/lennart/Documents/Axure/Prototypes/Axure%20for%20Mobile/resources/images/transpare
21
22    #javascript files
23    file:///Users/lennart/Documents/Axure/Prototypes/Axure%20for%20Mobile/resources/scripts/jquery-1
24    file:///Users/lennart/Documents/Axure/Prototypes/Axure%20for%20Mobile/resources/scripts/splitter
25    file:///Users/lennart/Documents/Axure/Prototypes/Axure%20for%20Mobile/resources/scripts/axutils.
26    file:///Users/lennart/Documents/Axure/Prototypes/Axure%20for%20Mobile/resources/scripts/axprotot
27    file:///Users/lennart/Documents/Axure/Prototypes/Axure%20for%20Mobile/resources/scripts/messagec
28    file:///Users/lennart/Documents/Axure/Prototypes/Axure%20for%20Mobile/data/configuration.js
29    file:///Users/lennart/Documents/Axure/Prototypes/Axure%20for%20Mobile/data/sitemap.js
30    file:///Users/lennart/Documents/Axure/Prototypes/Axure%20for%20Mobile/plugins/sitemap/sitemap.js
31    file:///Users/lennart/Documents/Axure/Prototypes/Axure%20for%20Mobile/plugins/page_notes/page_nc
32
```

Save this file as '`cache.manifest`' in your prototype's output directory.
To ensure that your manifest file is correct, check it on 'manifest-validator.com' [172].

Next, you want to add the manifest file to your prototype. Open the main HTML file of your prototype (not the '`index.html`' but the page you get when you close the sidebar), add one line at the top and change the '<html>' tag:

```
<!doctype html>
<html manifest="/cache.manifest">
```

Next, open a text editor, create a new file and enter this line of text:

```
AddType text/cache-manifest manifest
```

Save the file in the home directory of your prototype and name it '.htaccess'.

Now your prototype can be cached. Open it on your mobile, wait until it has been loaded, close it and turn on the mobile's 'Flight Mode'. Re-open the prototype and ignore the warning that there is no internet connection. You should now be able to view your prototype.

---

[1] If you want to find out more, Morten Hjerde has compiled an exhaustive list of fonts used on mobiles, [070]. Also a website dedicated to iOS fonts [071] exists.

[2] For free webfonts to include in your prototype take a look at Google's webfonts [072], at TypeKit [073] or Font Squirrel [074]. If you are are looking for (free) icon webfonts, check out www.weloveiconfonts.com [255].

[3] A similar example was presented by Paul Sharer in the Axure Forum [083].

[4] Kyle Adamo wrote an excellent tutorial on how to use Google Docs together with the Google Chart API [084] in Axure.

[5] For more information on the HTML5 support of mobile platforms in general take a look at this Wikipedia entry [085] and 'The State of HTML5 Video' [086]. For more information on iOS 'video' tag restrictions take a look at the official documentation [087] and at a blog post by Miller H. Borges Medeiros called 'Unsolved HTML5 Video Issues on iOS' [088].

[6] Thanks to Peter Gasston [089] for describing this JavaScript work-around.

[7] For more information see the MSDN page on Web Development for Mobile Phone: 'Supported Standards and Technologies' [090].

[8] See Wikipedia for more information on the Theora file [091] format.

[9] Please, get a decent browser. Seriously!

[10] There is a Wikipedia article with more information on HTML5 caching [094].

11. Adaptive Views

Axure 7.0 allows you to prototype responsive websites. You can use new *events* and *variables* to detect when the screen resolution changes and tell your prototype to update its content accordingly.

Adaptive and Responsive Web Design

Responsive Web Design (RWD) is the trending topic in web design today. There are long discussions on what it is, what it should be and how to build it. There is also disagreement on whether responsive design is part of adaptive design or vice versa.

Here is a definition from Aaron Gustafson (from an article well worth reading):

> "Responsive web design, as coined by Ethan Marcotte, means fluid grids, fluid images/media & media queries. Adaptive web design, as I use it, is about creating interfaces that adapt to the user's capabilities (in terms of both form and function). To me, adaptive web design is just another term for progressive enhancement of which responsive web design can (an often should) be an integral part, but is a more holistic approach to web design […]."

Aaron Gustafson
On Adaptive vs. Responsive Web Design [165]

So, adaptive web design is about creating web sites that adjust themselves to the capabilities of the device it is being viewed on.[1] It's up to you to decide what types of devices and capabilities your prototype should react to and how the layout and the functionality of your web site should adapt.

You might ask yourself why use a prototyping tool like Axure to create adaptive websites? Why not design directly in HTML, instead? Well, this depends on your personal preferences and skills. If you are comfortable with writing HTML and CSS code, go ahead. After all, you can use the 'real material' to build your design. If you align with the involved developers (on what frameworks to use) they'll be able to reuse your code. But if you're not really fluent with HTML and CSS, I think Axure is a good alternative. It allows you to create adaptive prototypes without any coding skills.

Since adaptive web design fundamentally changed the way websites are built, people have adjusted their workflow and came up with new tools and deliverables for this task. For example, Leigh Howells' article 'Wireframing for Responsive Design' [195] and Viljami Salminen's 'Responsive Workflow' [194] explain how adaptive design changed their way of working. Other must-reads are 'Responsive Navigation Pattern' [196] and 'Complex Navigation Pattern for Responsive Design' [197] by Brad Frost, where he explains how content and navigational elements can be adjusted to the screen size. Zurb offers free sketching templates [198] for your responsive design projects. And another great deliverable to showcase the visual design of your website are style tiles:

> "Style Tiles are a design deliverable consisting of fonts, colors and interface elements that communicate the essence of a visual brand for the web. They help form a common visual language between the designers and the stakeholders and provide a catalyst for discussions around the preferences and goals of the client. Style Tiles are similar to the paint chips and fabric swatches an interior designer gets approval on before designing a room."

> http://styletil.es/ [230]

For more information on style tiles read Samantha Warren's article 'Style Tiles and How They Work' [193].

An alternative to style tiles are style prototypes [243]. They use HTML to describe the "site colors, typography, button styles, rollovers, photography styles and other necessary elements to establish a website's proposed design direction". This deliverable can also be created in Axure.

How Axure Goes Adaptive

Axure's adaptive layout approach is currently unique. It allows you to define breakpoints (browser width/height values) for different resolutions. **While some properties of your UI elements are fixed** (text, *interactions*, disabled by default)**, others are adaptive** (location, size, color, *style* and *interaction styles*) and can be changed for each view. The benefit of this approach is that the UI elements you use are the same across different resolutions. Other prototyping tools merely create a copy of all your elements every time you define a new breakpoint.

In the following sections you will learn how to set up breakpoints, how to layout your screens and how to view adaptive prototypes.

Defining Breakpoints

You start by defining your 'base' resolution. Depending on your preferences you can choose a mobile-first approach (see the 'Mobile Constraints' chapter for more information) starting with a small screen size or pick a larger one (desktop or tablet-first).[2] This resolution will be the default one for your prototype. After you decided on your base view, define the breakpoints of your prototype. Click on the little icon next to the tab bar to open the 'Manage Adaptive View' popup.

Press the 'plus' button and set your first breakpoint. Name it and define the *condition* for its width and/or size values.

In this dialog you can also define if the adaptive properties should be inherited from another view. If you are using a mobile-first approach, use the 'greater than or equals' *condition* (and add one pixel to the width, as shown above) and build your way up. If you want to do it the other way around, Axure offers you several presets. In the screenshot above you see how to define a breakpoint for an retina iPhone screen in portrait-mode (640px width).

The inheritance dropdown allows you to define whether your elements shall inherit their adaptive properties (location, size, color, *style* and *interaction styles*) from another view.

Here is a set of typical mobile breakpoints starting from a mobile resolution where each view inherits its properties from a smaller one. The inheritance is indicated through indentation:

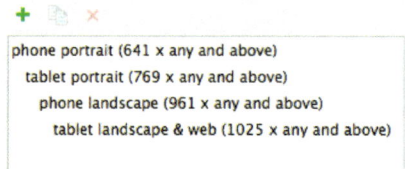

Note: Check your breakpoints before closing the dialog, it's very easy to pick the wrong *condition* in the dropdown and create ambiguous breakpoints .

After you close the dialog use the adaptive view tab bar to toggle between your views.

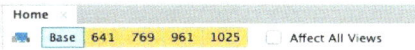

Building Your Prototype

Once you have defined the breakpoints for your prototype, start to layout your screen in its *base* view. When you are done, go through the different views and update your UI elements.

You'll most likely build one view after the other. But sometimes it makes sense to go back and forth between your largest and smallest view to determine how the website's content and navigation have to adapt to both extremes. But keep in mind that your prototype will use the *base* layout if no other *breakpoints* apply.

 Note: To center-align the content in your views, open the 'Page Style' tab and set the 'Page Align' property to 'center'. You have to set this in each view.

Page Guides and Breakpoints

If you open a view you'll notice that Axure added fixed *page guides* to indicate the breakpoints you defined. Unfortunately these *guides* are only helpful if you used a 'less than' *condition* to define your view. Thus I recommend adding your own *guides* to mark the screen estate if you used 'greater than' *conditions*.

Updating UI Elements

All you need to do now is to adjust the adaptive properties (location, size, color, *style* and *interaction styles*) of the UI elements in your views. The property presets for each view are inherited from its 'parent'. If you want to adjust a property in all views select the 'Affect all Views' checkbox.

Adaptive Masters

If you create *masters* in your prototype you will be able to layout them for the different views.

Replacing Elements

Sometimes you want to use a different representation for a certain UI element because it is better suited for the current view (e.g. your links to sub-pages were in a dropdown in the mobile view but in a tablet view you want them to be displayed as tabs). If this is the case, you can 'unplace' elements from view via the right-click context menu. These elements will become invisible and be marked in red in the 'Widget Manager'. There you can also 're-place' them again. Unplacing is different from using *hide/show actions*, which are used to build *interactions*. Since Axure doesn't know what UI element replaces the one you removed from view you have to define the *interactions* of the new element yourself.

Viewing Adaptive Prototypes

While creating your different views you'll want to see and compare them. You can resize your browser window by hand, use a browser-plugin (e.g. ResponsiView [199] for Chrome, FireSizer [200] for Firefox or ResponsiveResize [201] for Safari) or use ami.responsivedesign.is [251] to review your online prototypes.

---

[1] For an overview over different RWD examples take a look at mediaqueri.es [092]. They display screenshots of sites in different resolutions.

[2] For more information on the pros and cons of the different approaches, take a look this Forbes' article 'Forget Mobile First, Think Tablet First' [093].

12. Creating Documentation

In this chapter you'll learn how to create specification documents for your prototypes. You will learn how to make documentation mobile-friendly and how to create different types of documents.

Mobile UI Spec Settings

One of the great features of Axure (Pro) is that it allows you to create a specification of your prototype. To see what this means, just open 'Publish > Generate Specification' (or press CMD+SHIFT+D on a Mac or F9 on a PC and click 'Generate').

Axure will now create a Word file and will try to open it. You will see a document containing screenshots of each *page* accompanied by additional information (depending on how much you documented in Axure – but more on this later).

Page-based Documentation

If you use the *page*-based approach to create your prototype the content will be OKish. But if you want to document a *panel*-based prototype you need to tweak the documentation settings a bit to create a decent specification.

Panel-based Documentation

Since your prototype only consists of a single *page* containing your main *dynamic panel* (which contains even more *dynamic panels*), the default structure of Axure's documentation creates too many chapter levels (one for each *dynamic panel*): Show a *page*'s content, next show all *masters* for this *page*, and lastly show all *dynamic panels* and their *states* for this *page*.

Thus I suggest setting up your own documentation structure. Instead of using the auto-generated 'Master List', use a set of manually created *pages* to document your mobile prototypes. There are several advantages to this approach:

- It allows you to annotate the screen (e.g. add a device outline, use explanation bubbles, etc.).
- You can easily add 'special' *pages* like UI Flows to your documentation.
- Since you use *pages* for documenting, the specification structure is more visible in your Axure file (in the *sitemap*, that is) – otherwise it would be hidden inside the 'Generate Specification' settings.

This is how you set-up your specification structure: First, create a new top-level *page* (or *folder*) called 'Specification' and create *sub-pages* for the screens you want to document.

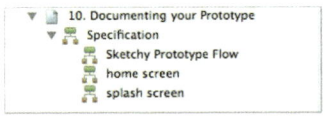

To distinguish them visually from 'regular' prototype *pages* set the diagram type to 'Flow' (select the *pages* in the *sitemap* > right-click > Diagram Type > Flow).

Next, turn all relevant 'screens' of your prototype into *masters* (if you haven't done so already) and drag them onto the *pages* you created. If you want to give your screens more 'context', add a device outline. You can also annotate them or put multiple screens on one *page* (e.g. create UI flows, show variants…).

Page Settings

Now click 'Generate Specification' (CMD+SHIFT+D on a Mac or F9 on a PC) and open the 'Pages' section. Uncheck the 'Section Header' checkmark to reduce the number of headings in your specification and disable the 'Include Sitemap List' setting because this is not needed for a *panel*-based prototype. Disable the 'Generate all Pages' setting and select the *pages* you want to include in your specification.

Master Settings

Open the 'Masters' section and disable the 'Include Master Section' setting, because you'll document *masters* differently. Check 'Document Masters in Pages Section' to have the *masters'* content documented.

 Note: Depending on how you documented your *masters* you might want to check 'Exclude Master Notes'. If it is not checked, the *page notes* (please read the next section for an explanation of what these are) will be displayed on each page. I usually exclude them because I only use *notes* to document *pages*.

With this, the basic specification structure for a *panel*-based prototype is in place, allowing you to document the (key) screens of your prototype.

What to Document

Before you start creating a prototype you should briefly consider what you want to document. The two 'objects' that Axure can create documentation for are *pages* and widget (your UI elements). You can give these objects any attribute you want. For *pages* the attributes are called 'notes', for *widgets* they are called 'fields'.

Axure already comes with some defaults. Decide which fields you want to use in your specification, delete the ones you don't need and add your own.

Documenting Pages

To define *page notes* click on the 'Manage Notes' link in the 'Page Properties' section. After you have updated the categories you will find them in the *'Page Notes'* tab in the drop down. To document screens I usually use the following *page note* fields:

- **Description**. One or two sentences explaining the purpose of the screen.
- **Interactions**. A couple of bullet points describing what you can do on the screen.

- **Open Issues**. Room to note down what still needs to be included in the interaction, the visual design, etc.
- **Notes**. A place for everything else.

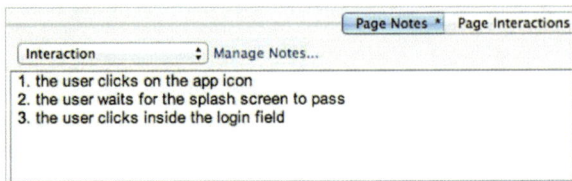

To see your *notes* as chapter headers in your specification, set the 'Show Notes Names as Header' checkmark in the 'Page Properties' section.

Documenting Widgets

To define your *widget notes* open the 'Widget Notes' tab in the interactions panel. Click the 'Customize' link to edit the existing *notes*.
If I document *widgets*, I use the following *note fields*:

- **Type** (a list containing entries like: button, checkbox, link, etc.)
- **Description**
- **Requirement ID**
- **Error ID**.

Afterwards, define how the *notes* will be displayed in your specification (Generate Specification > Widget Properties). By default a single table is created containing the *note fields* you defined.

 Note: You can define more than one table containing your *widget notes* by clicking the 'Add' link. I sometimes use a second table to create a wording list. Below is the screenshot of my wording list settings.

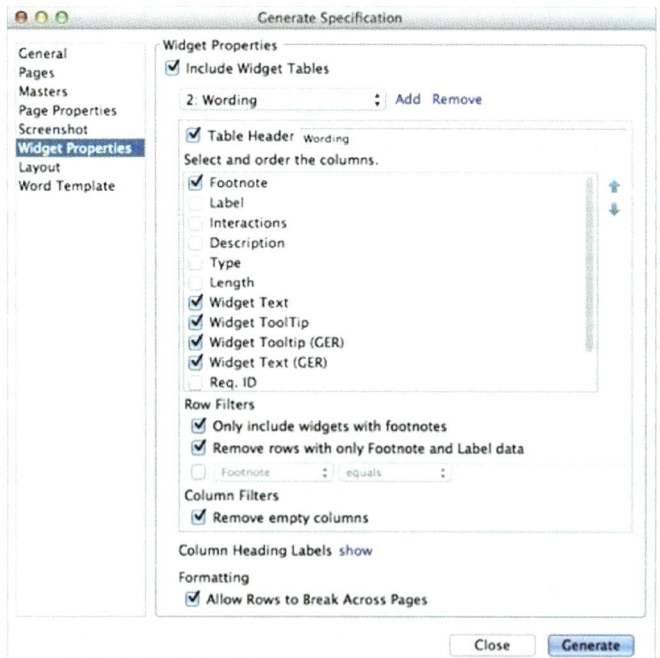

To reduce the number of empty rows set all the checkmarks in the 'Row Filters'. You might also want to enable the 'Column Filter' setting to further reduce your table's content. Depending on the size of your *widget* tables consider checking the 'Allow Rows to Break Across Pages' checkbox.

Screenshot Settings

To reduce the number of chapters I usually uncheck the 'Screenshot Header' checkbox in the 'Screenshot' (Generate Specification > Screenshot) section.

To have a cleaner layout tick the 'Put border on screenshot' checkbox and to see your *inline frame's* content tick 'Show default pages in Inline Frames'.

If you don't document your *widgets* you can uncheck 'Show footnotes on screenshot'. If you do, no yellow counters will be shown on the screenshots.

Adaptive View Settings

The 'Adaptive View' settings of Axure are quite basic. You can only define which *views* are to be included as screenshots. All *views* are included by default. In your specification each screenshot gets a header with the *view's* name.

Adjusting the Page Layout

Axure uses a single column layout by default (showing a screenshot on top and the information you defined below). This is fine for pad-based prototypes. But a two-column landscape layout is better suited for phone UIs (showing the image on the left and the description on the right).

To adjust the layout open the 'Generate Specification > Word Template' section and click on the 'Edit' link. In Word select 'File > Page Setup' and set the orientation to landscape. Save and close.

Back in Axure, open the 'Layout' section, select the 'Two Column' layout and reorder the entries via the arrow buttons. When you are done, the 'Screenshot' entry should be at the top, followed by the 'Column Break' entry. Sort the other categories to your liking.

Depending on your prototype's screen size you might want to reduce the percentage for the 'Left Column Width' to 30% or 40%.

Interaction Documentation

As I prefer not to document the *interactions* of my prototype (i.e. the *cases* and *actions* you defined in your prototype), I'll briefly explain how to disable them: Uncheck the 'Include Page Interactions' checkbox in the 'Page Properties' section and uncheck the 'Interactions' checkbox in 'Widget Properties'.

Adjusting the Template

If you want to adjust the overall layout of you specification (e.g. adding a custom header, adjusting font sizes, etc.) you have to edit Axure's Word template (Generate Specification > Word Template > Edit).

Start by generating a specification for a prototype and edit the styles inside the created document.[1] Starting from a 'vanilla' spec will give you a better picture of the content Axure creates and how your style changes will look. When you are done, save it and import it as the new template file.

Another thing you might want to do is add extra content to your specification, for example a 'Document Control' page or a 'Revision History' table. To do this, add the content inside the page template before or after the '[[INSERT AXURE SPEC]]' tag and add separate it by page breaks.

For more information on Axure's specification settings take a look at Luke Perman's talk at the Axure World 2009 [222] and his blog post [223] about the same topic.

With your specification structure in place you can now start to document your prototype. In addition to 'regular' documentation pages you might want to create some additional ones, like IA Diagrams, Use Case Diagrams, UI Flows and Contact Prints. I will explain how to create these in the following chapters.

IA Diagrams

With Axure you can quickly create an Information Architecture diagram. Use it to provide an overview of your app's or website's structure.

To create one simply drag-and-drop *pages* from Axure's s*itemap* onto the canvas. This results in a *rectangle* (with the *page* title) with a built-in link to the *page*. Change the shape by clicking the grey round circle or via the context menu (right-click > Select Shape). You can also auto-generate a page map by right-clicking on a *page* and selecting 'Generate Flow Diagram'. If you use a *panel*-based prototype use the individual *pages* of your specification in your IA diagram.

For more information see Axure's article 'Document processes with Flow Diagrams' [181].

Use Case Diagrams and Flows

If you want to create UML-style use case diagrams or flows charts you can use Axure's flow library, which contains a set of shapes (and an *image widget*) that offer blue anchors to connect lines to. Switch to the 'Connector Mode', to draw connecting lines.

Axure allows you to change the line color, width, pattern and the arrow style for your connectors.

 Note: If you include diagram pages in your specification I recommend that you manually edit the page after your specification is generated. If you use a two-column layout, set the layout to 'one-column' for each diagram page and manually scale the image to span across the whole page.

For an introduction to different chart formats please read Mike Hughes' article 'Visual Methods of Communicating Structure, Relationship, and Flow' [182]. For more information on UML-style Use Case diagrams check out Scott W. Ambler's article 'UML 2 Use Case Diagrams' [183], 'Writing Effective Use Case and User Story Examples' [252] and 'Applying Lessons from UML to UX' [184] by Peter Hornsby. For more information on see Axure's article 'Document processes with Flow Diagrams' [181].

User Interface Flows

UI flows (which are sometimes called storyboards) are a set of wireframes visualizing an 'interaction path' showing how the user gets from A to B.

Creating one in Axure is rather simple. If you turned your key screens into *masters* you can just drag them onto an empty page and place a transparent *rectangle* (in your screen size) from Axure's 'Flow' library on top of each screen (to get the blue connectors to attach the connector lines to). You can also use images instead of *masters* by using *image widget* from the 'Flow' library (they also come with connectors).

 Note: To get images from your prototype's screens you can use the 'Export [Page/Master] to Image' or the 'Export all Pages to Image' function in Axure's file menu.

You might want to add a device outline around your screens to provide more context.

Contact Prints

To review the entire design of an app or a website, use a 'contact print'.[2] It contains all the screens of your prototype in a grid view. It helps you find inconsistencies and common patterns in your screens. Just place all your key screens and their variances on a single page.

---

[1] For more information on editing Word document styles take a look at this Productivity Hub article 'View and edit styles quickly in Word 2010' [100].

[2] Yes, I stole the term from photography. See Wikipedia for more details on contact prints [101].

Appendix I – Best Practices

This chapter offers you best practices which will make your prototyping life easier.

Give Everything a Name

Everything! I am serious. Always name the following elements:

- *widgets*
- *dynamic panel states*
- *interaction cases* (of *widgets* and *pages).*

This allows you to identify and differentiate your elements when defining *interactions.* If you don't name them, you'll be amazed at how confusing your prototypes will become after a little while.

You can use a sophisticated naming scheme for your elements but I am quite pragmatic (read: 'lazy') about it:

- Only label key elements – i.e. elements that will be used in *interactions*, like textfields, buttons and overlays.
- Use a CamelCase [227] syntax for your labels. Describe the element's location, function, and the type. This allows you to easily identify your elements: e.g. 'loginSubmitBTN' is the submit button of your login form.
- Be consistent in your labeling. Don't use different abbreviations, or you won't be able to search for your elements.
- If an UI element is part of a *dynamic panel* and if the *interaction* is defined on this *panel* and not on the UI element, label the *panel*, not the UI element. It's about identifying elements that have *interactions* tied to it, not about correctness.
- If a *dynamic panel* has only a single *state*, give the *panel* and its *state* the same name.

If you follow these rules, working with UI elements will become much easier: You can now use the search field in the 'Case Editor' and check its 'hide unnamed' elements checkbox to filter out the unimportant elements.

Create Masters

If you are lazy and want to save yourself some effort in the long run, turn everything that you use more than once into a *master*. Turn both screen components as well as full screens into *masters*.

Another candidate for *masters* are key screens. If you turn them into *masters* you can easily create UI Flows (see 'User Interface Flows') with them or reuse them in different parts of your prototype.

I recommend creating two folders in your 'Masters' section, one called 'Screen Elements' and one called 'Key Screens' to structure your *master* section a bit.

Don't Combine Actions

Axure allows you to perform multiple *actions* in one line. If you do more complex prototypes you might need to set multiple *dynamic panels states* in one *case*. Axure allows you to multi-select *panels* and combine them into a single *action* (the image below is a screenshot of one of my prototypes. Impressively bad practice).

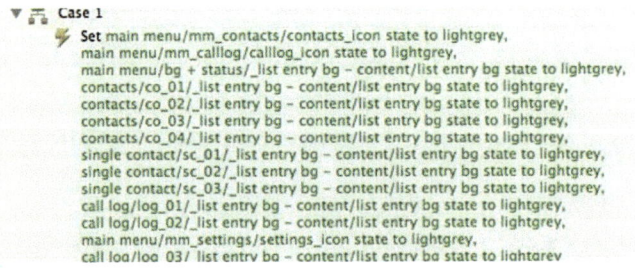

If you need to reorder these *actions* at some point – you can't, since they are now this big blob of text. Create a single entry for each *action* instead. Now each *action* can be moved around, copied and deleted.

Give Actions Enough Time

Every time you use an animation or a transition *action*, add a 'Wait' *action* with a similar timespan below.

This ensures that the prototype doesn't start doing something else (e.g. open a new *page*) before the animation is completed.

The Order of Your Actions

Remember that the order of your *actions* inside a *case* is important as well. They are processed one after the other. Statements following an *action* that changes your screen (e.g. 'Open Link in Current Window' or changing the *state* of the visible *panel*) will be not executed.

Check Your IFs And ELSEs

A common cause of error is forgetting to toggle an IF into an ELSE clause (via the right-click menu) or vice versa. Since they can't be visual differentiated it's easy to overlook them. Check which *cases* need to be exclusive (use an ELSE) and which are not (use an IF). This is important because each IF *clause* of an *event* will be evaluated. Review your *cases* every time you drag or copy-and-paste them.

Let me show you the implications – take a look at a typical IF-ELSE statement below.

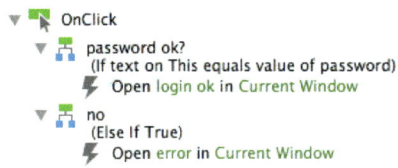

This can be described with the following flow diagram:

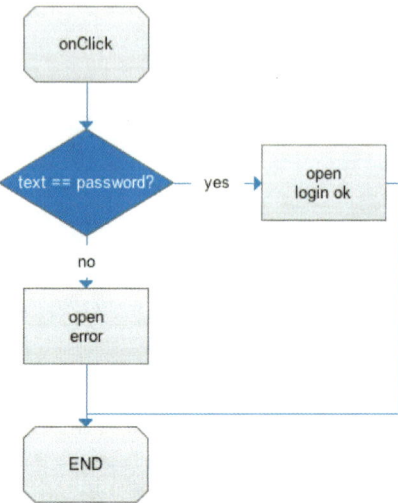

As you can see, only one of the *cases* will be visited. If you want to add another *condition* to be evaluated (before or afterwards), you need to add a third *case* starting with an IF *condition*:

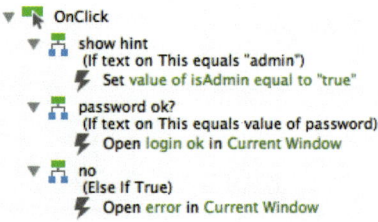

This set of *cases* translates into the following diagram:

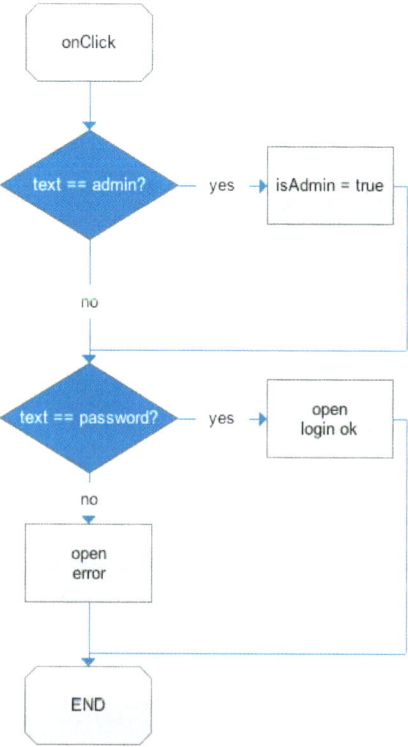

You can see that each IF *case* gets evaluated.

Last but not least, let me show you how a more complex, real world *case* looks (these are the *cases* used in the 'Scroll Detector'):

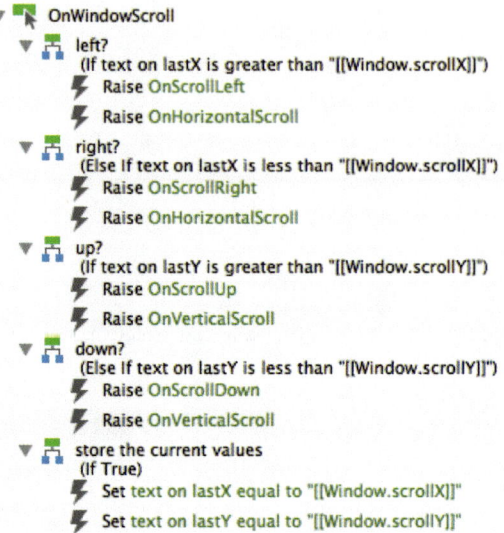

Try to sketch the diagram yourself…

Note that the last *case* (which will always be visited automatically) gets an 'IF True' *condition.*

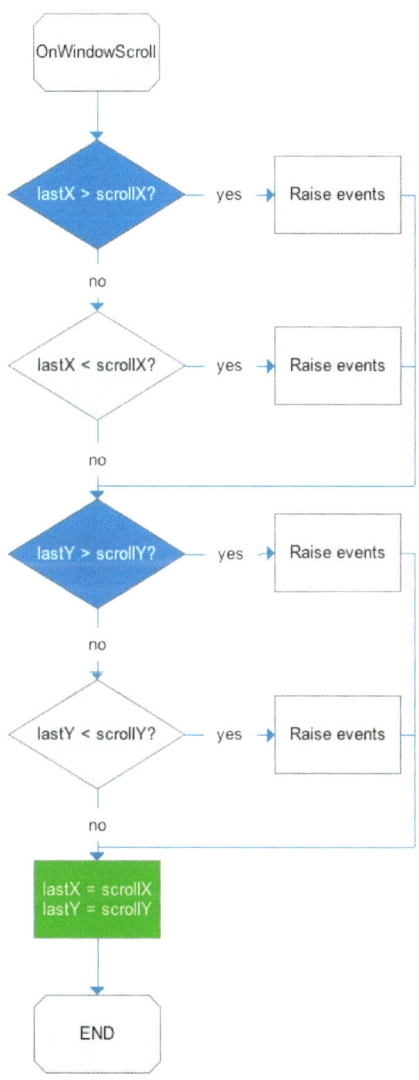

Simplify Your IF / ELSE Statements

Once you have built a prototype, go through its *interactions* trying to simplify its *cases*. Good candidates are instances where you use the same *actions* inside multiple *cases*. After a good night's sleep you will find something to take away – trust me. You might ask: 'Why bother?' – to have less and cleaner *interactions,* to reduce causes for error, you name it...

Initialize Your Variables

With Axure 7.0 you can initialize your *variables* (Project > Global Variable). Initialize all of them with a default value.

Use UI Elements' Real Sizes

Always use the correct dimensions of the UI elements in your prototype. If you don't, you probably have to re-layout your screens later on.

Use Interaction Styles

A feature that is often overlooked is the range of styles you can apply to elements based on their *state*:

- MouseOver
- MouseDown (not needed for mobile)
- Selected
- Disabled.

Use these to visualize the different *state*s of your UI elements. Click on the links in the 'Widget Properties' tab to edit them.

Use Custom Styles

An even more powerful (and overlooked) feature is that you can define your own *styles* for *widgets* and *pages* – plus you can edit the default *styles*. Create *custom styles* to be able to update the layout of your UI elements across *pages*, *panels* and *masters*.

If you select a *widget* and open the 'Widget Style' section you'll see a dropdown showing the element's active *style*. Open the 'Widget Style Editor' by clicking the button next to it.

In the 'Custom' tab you can add your own *style* definitions. You can define for example different button styles. If you edit a *style*, the change will be applied to all elements that share the *style* – even to *masters*. The same logic applies to *page* styles.

Appendix II – Tips and Tricks

This chapter contains advice on how to work faster and how to be more efficient with Axure.

Save! Save! Save!

You don't want to lose work. Activate 'Auto-Save' under 'File > Backup Settings'. The lowest amount you can enter there is five minutes. If you want to save more frequent than this (and you are working on a Mac) you can use an auto-save script [186] created by Paul Sharer. And make it a habit to save (CMD+S on a Mac, CTRL+S on Windows) each time before creating a new prototype.

Know Your Shortcuts

Knowing Axure's keyboard shortcuts [260] will make you much faster. Here are a few essential ones:

- Hold the SHIFT-key for proportional scaling.
- Hold the ALT-key and drag a *widget* to create a copy of it.
- Hold the CMD-key on Mac to rotate *widgets* via the mouse (click on one of the element's corners).
- Using the cursor keys when holding down SHIFT will move an element according to your *grid settings* (usually by 10 pixels).
- You can TAB through the elements on a *page*.

Use the Position And Size Fields

Instead of using the mouse to drag elements around and resize them use the four entry fields Axure provides in the toolbar. Press CTRL+L to focus the first field on a PC and CMD+4 on a Mac. Use the TAB-key to navigate back (with SHIFT) and forth between the fields.

How to Click Through Elements

When you have a lot of elements stacked on top of each other you can click through them. Click on the top one, wait a short amount of time and click again. Repeat until you have reached the element you wanted to access.

Resize the Case Editor

For some reason the default size of the 'Case Editor' window is too small. Resize it to make the all *actions* visible. Since the window remembers its size you only have to do this once.

Check Your Variable's Values

Create a prototype with the *sitemap* visible (Publish > Generate HTML Files). Click the 'X=' icon above the *sitemap* to view the values of your *variables*.

Debugging Your Cases

Unfortunately there is no easy way to debug your prototypes, but one way to track down an error is to create a specification that includes all *interactions* and search within it (e.g. for unused *actions*).

To include the prototype's *interaction* you need to tick the following checkboxes in the 'Generate Specification' dialog (F9 on Windows or CMD+SHIFT+D on a Mac):

- 'Include Page Interaction' in the 'Page Properties' section
- 'Interactions' in the 'Widget Properties' section
- 'Generate all Pages' in the 'Pages' section
- 'Generate all Master' in the 'Masters' section.

Now you can review the *interactions* inside the Word specification.

Determine Your Screen Size

You can easily determine your current resolution using some of Axure's new *events* and *variables*. Let's create an element that always displays the current width and height in the bottom-right corner of your browser window.

Drag a *rectangle* on your canvas, label it (e.g. 'resolutionTracker') and right-click to turn it into a *dynamic panel*. Select 'Pin to browser' and tell it to stay in the bottom-right corner.

Next, turn it into a *master* to use its *page events* to update its text (yes, *masters* get their 'own' *page events*). Right-click on the *rectangle*, convert it into a *master* and double-click to open it. Add a new *case* to its 'OnPageLoad' *event* to initially display your window's width and height. Use the 'Set Text' *action* and assign '([[Window.width]]: [[Window.height]])' to it.

Close the 'Case Editor' and copy & paste the *case* you just built to the 'OnWindowResize' *event* of the *master*. Now the text will be updated after every screen resolution change. The resulting *cases* should look like this:

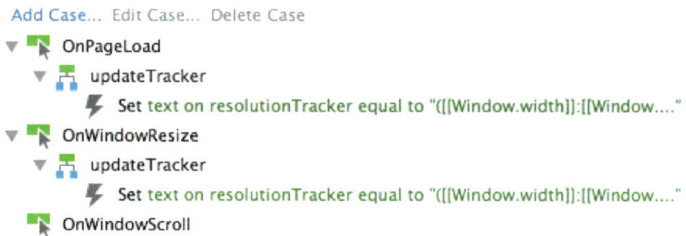

Close the *master* and preview your prototype. It should display something like this in its bottom-right corner:

Detect Scrolling

Let me show you how to build an element that notifies you when a *page* or *panel* has been scrolled. We'll be using the new 'OnWindowScroll' *event* that Axure added to *pages* and *masters*. Since it does not tell you in what direction the user scrolls, we'll create our own *events* to provide us this information.

First, press the 'Add Master' button in the *masters* section to create a new one. Drag a two *rectangle*s on the canvas, size them 50x50px and place them next to each other. You'll be using these two *rectangles* to store the current x and y value of you window's content. Name the two *rectangles* 'lastX' and 'lastY'.

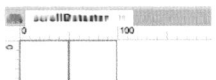

   Note: You could have used *variables* to store the values, but then you need to remember to import the *variables* when you reuse the *master* in another project. By using *rectangles* you avoid this dependency.

Next, you want to determine in which direction the user has scrolled. Double-click on the 'OnWindowScroll' *event* of the *master* to create a new *action* and click the 'Add condition' button. Choose the 'text on widget' *condition* from the dropdown, select the 'lastX' *rectangle* and check whether it is greater than the value of '[[Window.scrollX]]'. If the user has scrolled to the left this *condition* becomes true.

To communicate this information you need to raise *events*. Pick the 'Raise Event' *action* from the list and create six new *events* (one for each direction, plus one for vertical and one for horizontal scrolling in general):

☐ OnVerticalScroll
☐ OnScrollUp
☐ OnScrollDown
☐ OnHorizontalScroll
☐ OnScrollLeft
☐ OnScrollRight

Select both the 'OnScrollLeft' and the 'OnHorizontalScroll' *event*. Name your case 'left' and the resulting *interaction* should look like this:

Copy and paste the *case*, change the *condition* to 'less than' and replace the 'OnScrollLeft' *event* with the 'OnScrollRight' *event*. Copy and paste both *cases*, change the *variable* value to '[[Window.ScrollY]]' and raise the 'up' and 'down' *events*. You should now have *cases* for all four directions.

Last but not least, you need to store the current x and y position (using the *rectangles*). Double-click on the 'OnWindowScroll' *event* to create a new *action* and set the text on the *rectangles* to the '[[Window.ScrollX]]' and '[[Window.ScrollY]]' *variables*.

After you close 'Condition Builder' dialog, right-click on the *interaction* and toggle the 'else if' to an 'if' *condition*, as, you always want to perform this *action* when the *event* has been called.

This is what the resulting *cases* should look like:

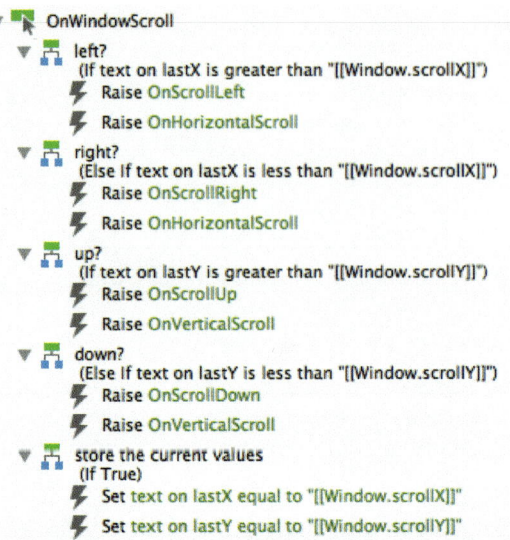

Now you only need to do some clean up: select the two *rectangles* and right-click to turn them into a *dynamic panel*. Hide the *panel* (since you don't want to see the x and y values in your prototype) and pin the *panel* (Widget Properties > Pin to browser) to the top-left corner. If you want to see the x and y values for debugging purposes toggle the *panel's* visibility.

If you close your *master,* drag it on to the canvas and click on its *widget interactions pane* you'll see the six *events* you just created:

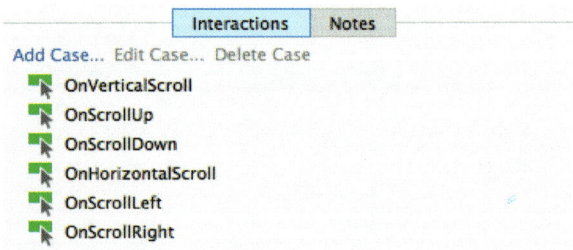

Now you can use these to tie *interactions* to the scrolling behavior in your prototype. To see it in action, visit the 'Fullscreen on Scroll' and the 'Sticky Headers for Lists' chapters.

Crazy Flicker

The so-called 'crazy flicker' is a *dynamic panel* that frequently raises an *event* thus allowing you to check or update your prototype. You can use it for example to detect a *variable* change or to create a timer.

The concept is quite simple: create a *dynamic panel* with two *states*, say 'a' and 'b'. On its 'OnPanelStateChange' *event* the *panel* waits a short time (e.g. 50ms), raises a *custom event* and then automatically changes its *state* to the next *one*.

Here is how to create a crazy flicker: Drag a new *dynamic panel* on the *page*, resize it to be (40x40px), give it two *states*: 'a' and 'b' and convert it to a *master* (right-click > Convert to Master) called '50msFlicker'. Open the *master* and double-click on its 'OnPanelStateChange' *event* to create a new *case*. Crete a new *event* called 'timeIsUp' and *raise* it, wait for 50ms and afterwards set the *panel* to its next *state* and loop.

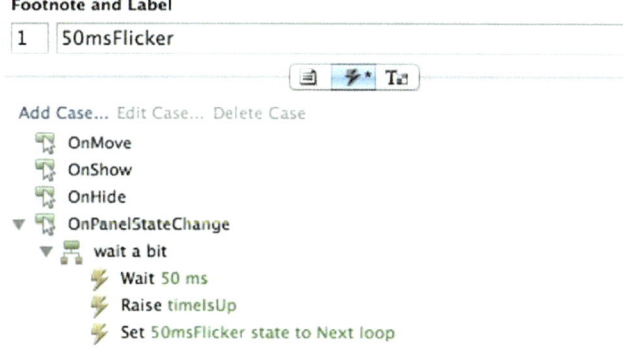

To automatically start the crazy flicker you need to change its *state* when the *master* is being loaded (via its 'Page Interactions' tab):

Now you can use the 'timeIsUp' *event* of the 'crazy flicker' in your prototypes.

Axure for Mobile, Second Edition

The Axure Source File

You can download the book's examples from this link:

`http://bit.ly/a4m_examples` (1.5mb)

Acknowledgements

This book would have never been written without the support from several people. First and foremost, I would like to thank my family, Steffi and Ida, for allowing me to write another edition of this book and putting up with me while I was writing it.

Next, I want to thank my editors: Maxi Freymann and Dirk Zimmermann for their invaluable advice and their patience – they often had to read and listen to the most half-baked ideas and still managed to give sensible advice; Daniel Becker, Thomas Glöckner and Jens Höbelheinrich for their thoughtful comments and feedback, and without Diana Wilson's excellent editing and proofreading skills the book wouldn't be nearly as readable as it is now. Thanks to Florian Simonis who created the book's cover art.

Thank you to all the readers of the first edition who asked questions, pointed out errors and provided feedback that helped me improve the content of this edition.

Last but not least a big thanks goes to the people at Axure, for creating my favorite prototyping toy and for their support and encouragement.

About the Author

Lennart Hennigs is a Senior User Experience Designer at Deutsche Telekom AG, where he designs web, mobile and fixed-line products. He has been designing and building products and services for over ten years.

Lennart studied Computer Science and Philosophy at the University of Paderborn. He is active in the German Chapter of the UPA and blogs and gives talks about User Experience topics – when he is not busy commuting.

Over the last couple of years he has grown very fond of Axure. He enjoys tinkering with it, pushing the tool to its limits when prototyping.

Follow @LennartHennigs on Twitter.

Printed in Great Britain
by Amazon.co.uk, Ltd.,
Marston Gate.